The Essential Buyer's Guide

LAND ROVER
SERIES III
1971 to 1985

Your marque expert:
Maurice Thurman

VELOCE PUBLISHING
THE PUBLISHER OF FINE AUTOMOTIVE BOOKS

The Essential Buyer's Guide Series

Alfa Romeo Alfasud (Metcalfe)
Alfa Romeo Alfetta: all saloon/sedan models 1972 to 1984 & coupé models 1974 to 1987 (Metcalfe)
Alfa Romeo Giulia GT Coupé (Booker)
Alfa Romeo Giulia Spider (Booker)
Audi TT (Davies)
Audi TT Mk2 2006 to 2014 (Durnan)
Austin-Healey Big Healeys (Trummel)
BMW Boxer Twins (Henshaw)
BMW E30 3 Series 1981 to 1994 (Hosier)
BMW GS (Henshaw)
BMW X5 (Saunders)
BMW Z3 Roadster (Fishwick)
BMW Z4: E85 Roadster and E86 Coupé including M and Alpina 2003 to 2009 (Smitheram)
BSA 350, 441 & 500 Singles (Henshaw)
BSA 500 & 650 Twins (Henshaw)
BSA Bantam (Henshaw)
Choosing, Using & Maintaining Your Electric Bicycle (Henshaw)
Citroën 2CV (Paxton)
Citroën DS & ID (Heilig)
Cobra Replicas (Ayre)
Corvette C2 Sting Ray 1963-1967 (Falconer)
Datsun 240Z 1969 to 1973 (Newlyn)
DeLorean DMC-12 1981 to 1983 (Williams)
Ducati Bevel Twins (Falloon)
Ducati Desmodue Twins (Falloon)
Ducati Desmoquattro Twins – 851, 888, 916, 996, 998, ST4 1988 to 2004 (Falloon)
Fiat 500 & 600 (Bobbitt)
Ford Capri (Paxton)
Ford Escort Mk1 & Mk2 (Williamson)
Ford Focus RS/ST 1st Generation (Williamson)
Ford Model A – All Models 1927 to 1931 (Buckley)
Ford Model T – All models 1909 to 1927 (Barker)
Ford Mustang – First Generation 1964 to 1973 (Cook)
Ford Mustang – Fifth Generation (2005-2014) (Cook)
Ford RS Cosworth Sierra & Escort (Williamson)
Harley-Davidson Big Twins (Henshaw)
Hillman Imp (Morgan)
Hinckley Triumph triples & fours 750, 900, 955, 1000, 1050, 1200 – 1991-2009 (Henshaw)
Honda CBR FireBlade (Henshaw)
Honda CBR600 Hurricane (Henshaw)
Honda SOHC Fours 1969-1984 (Henshaw)
Jaguar E-Type 3.8 & 4.2 litre (Crespin)
Jaguar E-type V12 5.3 litre (Crespin)
Jaguar Mark 1 & 2 (All models including Daimler 2.5-litre V8) 1955 to 1969 (Thorley)
Jaguar New XK 2005-2014 (Thorley)
Jaguar S-Type – 1999 to 2007 (Thorley)
Jaguar X-Type – 2001 to 2009 (Thorley)
Jaguar XJ-S (Crespin)
Jaguar XJ6, XJ8 & XJR (Thorley)
Jaguar XK 120, 140 & 150 (Thorley)
Jaguar XK8 & XKR (1996-2005) (Thorley)
Jaguar/Daimler XJ 1994-2003 (Crespin)
Jaguar/Daimler XJ40 (Crespin)
Jaguar/Daimler XJ6, XJ12 & Sovereign (Crespin)
Kawasaki Z1 & Z900 (Orritt)
Land Rover Discovery Series 1 (1989-1998) (Taylor)
Land Rover Discovery Series 2 (1998-2004) (Taylor)
Land Rover Series I, II & IIA (Thurman)
Land Rover Series III (Thurman)
Lotus Elan, S1 to Sprint and Plus 2 to Plus 2S 130/5 1962 to 1974 (Vale)
Lotus Europa, S1, S2, Twin-cam & Special 1966 to 1975 (Vale)
Lotus Seven replicas & Caterham 7: 1973-2013 (Hawkins)
Mazda MX-5 Miata (Mk1 1989-97 & Mk2 98-2001) (Crook)
Mazda RX-8 (Parish)
Mercedes-Benz 190: all 190 models (W201 series) 1982 to 1993 (Parish)
Mercedes-Benz 280-560SL & SLC (Bass)
Mercedes-Benz G-Wagen (Greene)

Mercedes-Benz Pagoda 230SL, 250SL & 280SL roadsters & coupés (Bass)
Mercedes-Benz S-Class W126 Series (Zoporowski)
Mercedes-Benz S-Class Second Generation W116 Series (Parish)
Mercedes-Benz SL R129-series 1989 to 2001 (Parish)
Mercedes-Benz SLK (Bass)
Mercedes-Benz W123 (Parish)
Mercedes-Benz W124 – All models 1984-1997 (Zoporowski)
MG Midget & A-H Sprite (Horler)
MG TD, TF & TF1500 (Jones)
MGA 1955-1962 (Crosier)
MGB & MGB GT (Williams)
MGF & MG TF (Hawkins)
Mini (Paxton)
Morgan Plus 4 (Benfield)
Morris Minor & 1000 (Newell)
Moto Guzzi 2-valve big twins (Falloon)
New Mini (Collins)
Norton Commando (Henshaw)
Peugeot 205 GTI (Blackburn)
Piaggio Scooters – all modern two-stroke & four-stroke automatic models 1991 to 2016 (Willis)
Porsche 356 (Johnson)
Porsche 911 (964) (Streather)
Porsche 911 (991) (Streather)
Porsche 911 (993) (Streather)
Porsche 911 (996) (Streather)
Porsche 911 (997) – Model years 2004 to 2009 (Streather)
Porsche 911 (997) – Second generation models 2009 to 2012 (Streather)
Porsche 911 Carrera 3.2 (Streather)
Porsche 911SC (Streather)
Porsche 924 – All models 1976 to 1988 (Hodgkins)
Porsche 928 (Hemmings)
Porsche 930 Turbo & 911 (930) Turbo (Streather)
Porsche 944 (Higgins)
Porsche 981 Boxster & Cayman (Streather)
Porsche 986 Boxster (Streather)
Porsche 987 Boxster and Cayman 1st generation (2005-2009) (Streather)
Porsche 987 Boxster and Cayman 2nd generation (2009-2012) (Streather)
Range Rover – First Generation models 1970 to 1996 (Taylor)
Range Rover – Second Generation 1994-2001 (Taylor)
Range Rover – Third Generation L322 (2002-2012) (Taylor)
Reliant Scimitar GTE (Payne)
Rolls-Royce Silver Shadow & Bentley T-Series (Bobbitt)
Rover 2000, 2200 & 3500 (Marrocco)
Royal Enfield Bullet (Henshaw)
Subaru Impreza (Hobbs)
Sunbeam Alpine (Barker)
Triumph 350 & 500 Twins (Henshaw)
Triumph Bonneville (Henshaw)
Triumph Herald & Vitesse (Ayre)
Triumph Spitfire and GT6 (Ayre)
Triumph Stag (Mort)
Triumph Thunderbird, Trophy & Tiger (Henshaw)
Triumph TR2 & TR3 - All models (including 3A & 3B) 1953 to 1962 (Conners)
Triumph TR4/4A & TR5/250 - All models 1961 to 1968 (Child & Battyll)
Triumph TR6 (Williams)
Triumph TR7 & TR8 (Williams)
Triumph Trident & BSA Rocket III (Rooke)
TVR Chimaera and Griffith (Kitchen)
TVR S-series (Kitchen)
Velocette 350 & 500 Singles 1946 to 1970 (Henshaw)
Vespa Scooters – Classic 2-stroke models 1960-2008 (Paxton)
Volkswagen Bus (Copping)
Volkswagen Transporter T4 (1990-2003) (Copping/Cservenka)
VW Golf GTI (Copping)
VW Beetle (Copping)
Volvo 700/900 Series (Beavis)
Volvo P1800/1800S, E & ES 1961 to 1973 (Murray)

www.veloce.co.uk

First published in June 2012, reprinted April 2018 and November 2019 by Veloce Publishing Limited, Veloce House, Parkway Farm Business Park, Middle Farm Way, Poundbury, Dorchester, Dorset, DT1 3AR, England.

Tel 01305 260068/Fax 01305 250479/e-mail info@veloce.co.uk/web www.veloce.co.uk or www.velocebooks.com.

ISBN: 978-1-787116-62-7 UPC: 6-36847-01662-3

Introduction & thanks
– the purpose of this book

This book provides a quick, step-by-step guide to selecting a Series III Land Rover that is appropriate for both your budget and your intended use.

Budgeting is important. This guide will help you avoid falling into the trap of buying the most expensive model you can afford, only to discover later that funds are not available to make the desired modifications or repairs. Costing of spares and repairs are outlined to assist you in deciding how authentic-to-year your budget allows your Land Rover to be.

A wide range of aftermarket accessories have been made available for Series III Land Rovers over the years; as a result, no two vehicles are the same. Many of these accessories are mentioned and commented upon within this guide.

You can best check current UK market prices in the classified sections of the three main Land Rover magazines: *Land Rover Owner International, Land Rover Monthly* and *Land Rover World*. These are available worldwide, but vehicle sales markets vary according to country; Series III Land Rovers are significantly more expensive in the USA than in the UK, and similarly in other countries, where there is strong collector interest. The vehicles are generally cheaper in developing countries, where you are likely to find they have been locally modified.

The plastic radiator grille is the most distinguishing feature of a Series III compared to Series I, II and IIA.

Don't be concerned that a seller may consider you as wasting their time if you thoroughly examine the vehicle and decide not to buy. You need to find the vehicle that is right for you. Don't expect to find it at the first attempt, and be prepared to travel long distances. Knowledge gained from reading this book should equip you with the most searching questions to ask over the phone or by email correspondence, thereby limiting unproductive journeys as much as possible.

Buying from a reputable dealer will be more expensive, but you get more guarantees of quality and a degree of redress if something goes wrong. The private seller cannot offer you the same degree of security; this book provides you with the basis for a more confident purchase.

Detailed advice and technical data has been included throughout, so that this guide can serve as a useful ongoing resource during vehicle ownership, too. Acknowledged vehicle weaknesses are also included, with the intention that the owner may manage the reliability of their vehicle more effectively.

Over half a million vehicles come within the scope of this guide, with the majority of those being originally exported from the UK. So, if you search, you can expect to find a Series III Land Rover in almost any corner of the world; many are in sleep mode however, awaiting a restoration project. Most overseas models were originally

Bob and Sarah's 109in Station Wagon. This model is considered by many to be the iconic Series III.

commissioned into police or army services. Many have since undergone multiple modifications more suited to the desires of civilian owners. This guide is intended to be of value in assessing these modified vehicles, too.

Thanks

Bob Lane and fiancée Sarah for allowing me repeated access to their fully-restored Series III (shown above), which has been a source for many photographs in this book.

Mustafa Haciahmetoğlu for providing photos of his 1974 Series III, featured on the cover.

Numerous owners of Series IIIs, some of whom are members of the Land Rover Series III, 90 & 110 Owners' Club. They have provided me with much information over the years whilst either attending or publicly displaying their vehicles at various Land Rover shows across the UK.

Headlamps in the wings don't always indicate a Series III; this is a late Series IIA model. Radiator grilles are distinctive though.

www.velocebooks.com / www.veloce.co.uk
Details of all current books • New book news • Special offers

Contents

The Essential Buyer's Guide™ currency
At the time of publication a BG unit of currency "●" equals approximately £1.00/US$1.22/Euro 1.11. Please adjust to suit current exchange rates.

1 Is it the right vehicle for you?
– marriage guidance

Tall & short drivers
Seats have very little adjustment; 'County' models have more adjustable and more comfortable seating. Drivers over 6ft (1.85m) have limited legroom, and upwards vision may be restricted in all models.

Controls
Unlike earlier Series models, there is synchromesh on all gears. Steering is heavy with all-terrain tyres (power steering kits can be fitted). 109in models have servo assisted brakes, whereas many 88in models don't, in which case the brake pedal requires firm pressure.

The driver's seat has very limited adjustment for legroom, and cushioning is basic.

Will it fit the garage?
Maximum dimensions are:

Model	Length	Width	Height (hood up)*
88in	11ft 11in (3.62m)	5ft 6in (1.69m)	6ft 6in (1.97m)
109in	14ft 7in (4.44m)	5ft 6in (1.69m)	6ft 6in (1.97m)

*fixed roof models are 1-2in (25mm-50mm) lower than hooded models, except the 12-seater Station Wagon, which is 1in (25mm) higher.

Interior space
Interior surfaces are vinyl, basic, rugged and pet-friendly, though later County models have cloth seating. Seating capacities range from two to twelve. Comfort is not an option on long journeys due to lack of legroom and the steep angular seat design. Even hardtop models allow for large load carrying capacity, due to foldable rear seats (if present) and large rear door or tailgate.

Usability
Outstanding off-road performance. Excellent load carrying ability. Requires dedication to the marque for long journeys in modern traffic. Petrol-

Customised windows can be quite easily incorporated into van sides if required.

engined models are more capable of towing, particularly the six-cylinder engine. The standard Zenith 36IV carburettor on the 2286cc engine can be swapped for a Weber 34ICH carburettor, which will improve economy at the expense of some power loss.

Running costs
These are thirsty vehicles, even if the engine is in good condition and well tuned, and especially true of the six-cylinder engine. Cheaper insurance is available from agents having specialist 4x4 sections. Only vehicles from the first year of production (1971) are exempt from road tax in the UK. Due to age, the vehicle will need more frequent servicing, but by doing it yourself (DIY) you can significantly reduce costs.

Parts availability
Parts are often available in countries whose police or army used Series Land Rovers. USA and Australasia have suppliers. Several UK companies with websites ship parts worldwide (see Chapter 16). Many parts are being remanufactured. Some six-cylinder engine parts are becoming harder to find.

The spare wheel takes up significant space if mounted inside the vehicle. Here's a better solution.

Plus points
Good towing and off-road driving capabilities. Very DIY-friendly, with a variety of maintenance/repair/ restoration manuals available. Relatively easy to convert to alternative fuels. Remanufactured engine upgrades are available.

Minus points
Front leaf springs dictate a large turning circle, particularly for long-wheelbase models – how tight is the turn into your driveway/garage? Realistic top speeds are 60mph (95km/h) and 50mph (80km/h) for petrol and diesel engined vehicles respectively, although six-cylinder petrol models have a top speed of 65mph (105km/h). Short-wheelbase models have a bouncy ride.

2 Cost considerations
– affordable, or a money pit?

Prices exclude taxes.

Mechanical parts

Brake shoes (x4)	●x50
Clutch plate	●x35
Alternator	●x36
Exhaust silencer	●x16
Flywheel	●x125
Fuel tank	●x58
~~Gasket set, engine~~	~~●x13~~
Gearbox mounting	●x2
Head gasket set	●x15
Hub bearing	●x8
Master cylinder kit	●x18
Outrigger, front	●x15
Propshafts SWB	●x51
Rear crossmember	●x104
Shock absorber	●x10
Starter motor brushes	●x6
Timing chain	●x15
Trackrod	●x36
Trackrod end	●x8
Water pump overhaul kit	●x9
Wheel bearing rear kit	●x12
Wiper blade	●x8
Wheel cylinder	●x13

Body parts

Bulkhead, galv	●x1035
Door hinge	●x7
Door bottom	●x52
Door pillar	●x47
Dumb iron, front	●x35
Footwell panel	●x23
Galv. chassis (SWB)	●x1180
Hood, full (SWB)	●x288
Hood stick set SWB	●x375
Lid for seatbox	●x16
Seat belts, pair	●x160
Seat 3-man bench	●x95
Wing outer	●x140

Many Series III parts are now remanufactured, but always try to get original manufacturer's (OEM) parts whenever possible.

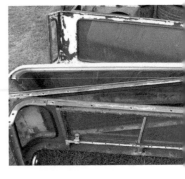

Used parts are readily available in the UK, and can also often be found in countries where the military used Series III vehicles.

It's common to find non-Land Rover engines fitted to Series III vehicles, so check on parts availability for any non-standard engine that has been fitted. Some parts for the 2.6-litre petrol engines are extremely hard to find, and others are expensive. In the UK and areas of Europe, most parts are available in used condition at considerably less cost than new or remanufactured parts. If model authenticity is not an issue, then repair costs can sometimes be reduced by substituting parts from earlier or later years; even those from Series IIA Land Rovers. In terms of fuel economy, engines are increasingly less economical in the order 2.25-litre diesel, 2.25-litre petrol and 2.6-litre petrol.

www.velocebooks.com / www.veloce.co.uk
Details of all current books • New book news • Special offers

3 Living with a Land Rover
– will you get along together?

The Land Rover was conceived as an all-purpose vehicle with significant DIY potential built-in, and this forms part of the vehicle's popular appeal. Only its predecessor, the Jeep, is also referred to commonly by its manufacturer's name, rather than simply as a 4x4. You will be buying into a living legend.

The youngest Series Land Rovers covered by this buyer's guide are over 25 years-old already. Your driving style will need to take a corresponding step backwards in time. The engine will struggle to keep up with modern traffic and may slow rapidly on hills. Say goodbye to concepts like reasonable acceleration, tight cornering, soft suspension, last minute braking, good fuel economy and parallel parking. The 109in models have very wide turning circles that may affect your ability to park the vehicle exactly where you wish to, or even limit the car parks you can use. Vehicle height may stop you using multi-story car parks, though the large turning circle would put most of those off limits anyway.

Correct procedures must be used for the controls to avoid serious damage to the transmission.

The six-cylinder engine is the only original option that allows you to reach 70mph (110 km/h). Be prepared to accept a more time-dilated mode of travel, with its accent upon the journey as much as the destination.

If fuel consumption is a major concern then the diesel engine options are best, though a sound insulation kit may be advisable to facilitate conversation on long hauls. The 2.25-litre diesel engine is under-powered; you really need to test drive it for suitability to your needs. Alternatively, the relative liveliness of the petrol engines can become more economical, on regular long journeys, with the fitting of an overdrive. Many owners have converted their vehicles to run with alternative engines having greater power and/or better fuel economy.

Volume-wise the vehicles are spacious, though life is cramped for passengers in a 12-seater Station Wagon. It's quite amazing what can pass through the rear door of a Series Land Rover; typically 42in (1.07m) by 34in (0.86m). Towing ability is excellent, albeit on the slow side, and steep inclines will not halt you.

The classic box-shaped body of the Land Rover enables larger loads to be carried.

Not everyone wishes to leave the road behind and head overland, but if you do, then it's worth bearing in mind that these vehicles were designed for farmer's fields. The short-wheelbase models are the preferred base vehicle for off-road competitive events, which stands as testimony to their inherent ability in this regard. Their potential for performance modification is also excellent. Each country has its own policy regarding the use of unsurfaced roads, and whilst a Series Land Rover will almost always get through, you should consider the legality of doing so. The UK, for example, is gradually restricting access to vehicles on 'green lanes,' and so 'pay-and-play' sites are becoming popular.

A well maintained Series III will bring pleasure to not only you, but many others who see it.

The design of the vehicle means that many modifications are possible. However, putting the spare wheel here adds stress to the front springs and restricts airflow.

If you're one of the increasing number of owners who wish to retain vehicle authenticity, then modifications may be considered off-limits. In such circumstances, you may find that living with a Series III is less demanding on the pocket than other, earlier models; the later the year, the more readily available the parts, and the more change you get back.

If, like myself, creature comforts are welcomed, then life with a Series Land Rover becomes more flexible. You can, for example, opt for a seating upgrade, fit a disc braking kit to make braking less of an effort, or otherwise modify the vehicle to suit your own particular needs. Some owners have even found ways to fit radios and can actually hear the music having fitted suitable sound insulation. Road-going tyres are much quieter than the off-road or all-terrain variety.

For cold climates, the standard heater in all models serves for the front seat passenger to warm their hands on and little else. If you live in a tropical climate, then the near vertical windscreen and steep vehicle sides keep the interior cooler than in many other, more modern, 4x4 vehicles – the natural flow of air through the gaps in the door and floor seals is not really a concern.

If you are mechanically minded, and can assemble flat-pack furniture without having bits left over, then you've already served a basic mechanical apprenticeship. Armed with one of the excellent workshop manuals available, you should be able to service and maintain your own vehicle. You need a minimum of specialist tools and equipment. Many owners get great pleasure and satisfaction from maintaining and/or modifying their vehicles. There is much additional assistance available, when required, from Land Rover clubs, websites and forums (see Chapter 17). Unlike ordinary cars, you should be able to crawl under all parts of a Series III Land Rover quite easily unaided. If you do take the DIY path, then it's important to realize that most of your classic vehicle's original parts are en-route to causing you trouble due to their age. Regular inspections will pick up those hardening rubber hoses, loose joints, and leaking seals, etc. Genuine replacement parts will enable you to reach your destination, but there are many poor quality, cheap alternatives that will bring your journey to a standstill – be warned!

It's not unusual for Series III models to have been assembled from different vehicles, and the legality of the final registered documents for the vehicle should be checked.

A Series III will allow you to reach isolated places that you could not hope to achieve in a single day on foot.

4 Relative values
– which model for you?

There is more detail on values in Chapter 12, but this chapter expresses, in percentages, the relative value of the individual models.

Series III 88in County Station Wagon 1982-1984
2286cc petrol engine **100%**
2286cc diesel engine **95%**

Series III 109in County Station Wagon 1982-1983
2286cc petrol engine **85%**
2286cc diesel engine **80%**

Series III 88in Station Wagon 1971-1984
2286cc petrol engine **80%**
2286cc diesel engine **75%**

Series III 88in truck cab 1971-1984
2286cc petrol engine **75%**
2286cc diesel engine **70%**

Series III 109in Station Wagon 1971-1984
2286cc petrol engine **70%**
2286cc diesel engine **65%**

Series III 109in Station Wagon 1971-1979
2625cc petrol engine **60%**

Series III 109in truck cab 1971-1983
2286cc petrol engine **55%**

Series III 109in truck cab 1971-1979
2625cc petrol engine **50%**

88in County Station Wagon displaying distinctive striping.

88in Safari Station Wagon with Safari roof.

Furthermore –
In the UK, for pre-1973 vehicles, at the time of publication of this guide, you can expect to pay say 5% more due to them being exempt from the annual road tax.

A well restored Series III displaying its original factory specifications could be a prize winning entry in show competitions, and could command the same price as a new small family car.

It's quite common to find that an alternative engine has been fitted to increase power and/or fuel economy.

109in Safari Station Wagon with Safari roof.

109in truck cab with soft top.

88in soft top.

Similarly, other modifications could have been carried out, such as an LPG conversion, alloy wheels, non-standard seats or chequer-plate body panels. These modifications all detract from original specification and often lower the maximum resale value of a refurbished vehicle.

Some countries, including the UK, allow only limited modifications to vehicles before they become subject to reappraisal for road tax purposes. A vehicle with unapproved modifications may not be worth much unless approval is granted, so check on the legal status of any modifications.

Interchangeability of parts between models means that part of the body may not be correct for the chassis number. Hybrid models are common, especially amongst vehicles that have been modified for off-road use, and their value often reflects their non-pedigree status.

Many Series III 'County' models are not original, and are actually vehicles retrofitted with County seating and markings. Original County models were only available in Russet Brown and Masai Red, with cream coloured striping. They cannot predate 1982.

www.velocebooks.com / www.veloce.co.uk
Details of all current books • New book news • Special offers

5 Before you view
– be well informed

To avoid a wasted journey, and the disappointment of finding that the vehicle does not match your expectations, it will help if you're very clear about what questions you want to ask before you pick up the telephone. Some of these points might appear basic, but when you're excited about the prospect of buying your dream classic, it's amazing how some of the most obvious things slip the mind ... Also check Land Rover magazines for the current values of the model you are interested in. These will contain price guides and auction results.

Where is the vehicle?
Is it going to be worth travelling to the next county/state, or even across a border? A locally advertised vehicle, although it may not sound very interesting, can add to your knowledge for very little effort, so make a visit – it might even be in better condition than expected.

Dealer or private sale?
Establish early on if the vehicle is being sold by its owner or by a trader. A private owner should have all the history, so don't be afraid to ask detailed questions. A dealer may have more limited knowledge of a vehicle's history, but should have some documentation. A dealer may offer a warranty/guarantee (ask for a printed copy) and finance.

Cost of collection & delivery?
A dealer may well be used to quoting for delivery by vehicle transporter. A private owner may agree to meet you halfway, but only agree to this after you have seen the vehicle at the vendor's address to validate the documents. Conversely, you could meet halfway and agree the sale, but insist on meeting at the vendor's address for the handover.

View – when & where?
It's always preferable to view at the vendors home or business premises. In the case of a private sale, the vehicle's documentation should tally with the vendor's name and address. Arrange to view only in daylight and avoid a wet day.

Reason for sale?
Do make it one of the first questions. Why is the vehicle being sold and how long has it been with the current owner? How many previous owners?

Left-hand drive to right-hand drive & special conversions
If a steering conversion has been carried out, it can only reduce the value and it may well be that other aspects of the vehicle still reflect the specification for a foreign market. If a bodywork or LPG conversion has been carried out, was it done professionally?

Condition (body/chassis/interior/mechanical)?
Ask for an honest appraisal of the vehicle's condition. Ask specifically about some of the check items described in Chapter 7.

All original specification?
An original equipment vehicle is invariably of higher value than a customised version.

Matching data/legal ownership
Do VIN/chassis, engine numbers and licence plate match the official registration document? Is the owner's name and address recorded in the official registration documents?

For those countries that require an annual test of roadworthiness, does the vehicle have a document showing it complies (an MOT certificate in the UK, which can be verified on 0300 123 9000 or gov.uk/check-mot-status)?

If a smog/emissions certificate is mandatory, does the vehicle have one?

If required, does the vehicle carry a current road fund license/licence plate tag?

Does the vendor own the vehicle outright? Money might be owed to a finance company or bank. The vehicle could even be stolen. Several organisations will supply ownership data, based on the vehicle's licence plate number, for a fee. Such companies can often also tell you whether the vehicle has been 'written-off' by an insurance company. In the UK these organisations can supply vehicle data:

DVSA 0300 123 9000　　DVLA 0844 453 0118
HPI 0113 222 2010　　AA 0800 056 8040
RAC 0330 159 0364

Other countries will have similar organisations.

Unleaded fuel
If necessary, has the vehicle been modified to run on unleaded fuel?

Insurance
Check with your existing insurer before setting out; your current policy might not cover you to drive the vehicle if you do purchase it.

How you can pay
A cheque/check will take several days to clear and the seller may prefer to sell to a cash buyer. However, a banker's draft (a cheque issued by a bank) is as good as cash, but safer, so contact your own bank and become familiar with the formalities that are necessary to obtain one.

Buying at auction?
If the intention is to buy at auction, see Chapter 10 for further advice.

Professional vehicle check (mechanical examination)
There are often marque/model specialists that will undertake professional examination of a vehicle on your behalf. Owners' clubs will be able to put you in touch with such specialists.

Other organisations that will carry out a general professional check in the UK are:
AA – 0800 056 8040 / www.theaa.com/vehicle-inspection (motoring organisation with vehicle inspectors)
RAC – 0330 159 0720 / www.rac.co.uk/buying-a-car/vehicle-inspections (motoring organisation with vehicle inspectors)
Other countries will have similar organisations.

6 Inspection equipment
– these items will really help

This book
Reading glasses (if you need them for close work)
Magnet (not powerful, a fridge magnet is ideal)
Torch
Probe (a small screwdriver works very well)
Overalls
Mirror on a stick
Digital camera
A friend, preferably a knowledgeable enthusiast

Before you rush out of the door, gather together a few items that will help as you work your way around the vehicle. This book is designed to be your guide at every step, so take it along and use the check boxes to help you assess each area of the vehicle you're interested in. Don't be afraid to let the seller see you using it.

Take your reading glasses if you need them to read documents and make close-up inspections.

A magnet will help you check if the steel parts of the vehicle are full of filler. Use the magnet to test door pillar and bulkhead areas, but be careful not to damage the paintwork. If the body panels have been repaired with filler then a magnet will not identify it, as they are made from an aluminium alloy. A torch with fresh batteries will be useful for peering into the wheelarches and under the vehicle. A torch where the beam can be focussed is the most useful.

A small screwdriver can be used – with care – as a probe, particularly on the chassis. With this you should be able to check an area of severe corrosion, but be careful – if it's really bad the screwdriver might go right through the metal!

Be prepared to get dirty. Take along a pair of overalls, if you have them. Fixing a mirror at an angle on the end of a stick may seem odd, but you'll probably need it to help you to peer into some of the important crevices.

If you have the use of a digital camera, take it along so that later you can study some areas of the vehicle more closely. Take a picture of any part of the vehicle that causes you concern, and seek a friend's opinion. Setting the camera to high resolution and subsequently transferring the image to a computer will enable you to view areas in great detail.

Ideally, have a friend or knowledgeable enthusiast accompany you – a second opinion is always valuable.

7 Fifteen minute evaluation
– walk away or stay?

If doors don't close easily, some adjustment is possible via the hinge mounting bolts.

Unlike earlier Series models, dash controls are more accessible to the driver.

How does it go/sound/feel?

Concentrate on checking for the problems that would trouble your wallet/purse the most. Find out from the seller what the vehicle has been used for previously. There are advantages to poking your head into the engine bay both before and after the test drive. When the engine is running, but still relatively cold, look for signs of a leaking water hose or a weeping radiator core. This is also the best time to check for a smokey exhaust and miscellaneous rattles. Check if there is an oil film visible in the radiator coolant; suggesting a damaged and leaking cylinder head gasket (don't remove the radiator cap when the engine is hot). After the test drive you will have a better idea of where the, almost inevitable, oil leaks are; decide for yourself whether they are significant and require urgent attention. The engine should idle smoothly, without slow, heavy knocking sounds from the bottom, or rapid, light chattering sounds from the top. The former would suggest worn engine bearings (bottom end), and the latter some rocker shaft component wear.

• Bottom end problems are best heard when the engine is rotating quite slowly. So, with handbrake on and the engine at a fast tickover, slowly engage the clutch and listen carefully until the engine almost stalls.

• Chattering sounds can be best located by using a wooden dowel or a stick as a stethoscope. If the stick leads you to the front engine cover, then worn timing chain rattle could be a problem. Be careful to avoid putting the stick in the area around the fan blades.

There should be no grey-blue or black smoke from the exhaust when the engine is revved. The former indicates combustion chamber wear, unless it occurs on start-up and when accelerating after over-run, in which case, it could be just valve stem oil seals leaking on a petrol engine. Black smoke from diesels indicates that the fuel-injection system may need tuning or parts replacing, whilst from petrol engines it will be a carburettor adjustment or wear problem. Acrid white smoke from a diesel engine indicates a combustion fault; possibly a coolant leak from a damaged cylinder head gasket.

If you are insured to drive the vehicle, take it for a short road test:

• When starting off, listen for any initial 'clunk' sound; indicating serious wear somewhere along the transmission line. If present, you'll need to try to locate the source later.

• The vehicle should drive straight 'hands-off' the steering wheel. A small amount of steering correction to maintain a straight line is common, but you should not need to correct the steering wheel by more than the distance across the fingers of one hand. There are six steering ball joints, and wear in any one of them will affect the steering.

• The vehicle should brake in a straight line. Some models have servo assisted brakes, but even then, brake pedal pressure is still high compared to modern cars. Early models have only a single line brake system. Post 1980, the front brakes on short-wheelbase models were enlarged to long-wheelbase specification.

• Try each gear for ease of use, and its ability to stay selected on over-run. If 2nd or 3rd gear jumps out on over-run, the selectors may be worn.

• Listen for gear chattering on over-run, indicating general wear in the gearbox. Don't expect a silent gearbox for this age of vehicle though, but gear changes should be smooth. All gears have synchromesh, but changes need to be slower than for modern gearboxes. Lack of sufficient oil can make the gearbox noisy. It's common for oil to pass through a worn seal between the main gearbox and the transfer box, resulting in the transfer box being overfull.

• Check reverse gear – you need to give the gearlever a firm nudge to select reverse.

• If an overdrive has been fitted, try it out in third and fourth gears, if road conditions permit.

• Find some soft ground, preferably with a loose or gravel surface, to try the four-wheel drive and verify that it works. You won't know for sure whether the front wheels are driving unless they slip on the surface.

By checking the four-wheel drive you will also discover if the rear differential has been swapped for a more motorway-friendly version – the vehicle will handle like a wild stallion if it has,

Engaging the freewheel hubs (if fitted) will enable the four-wheel drive to be tested, and also help identify any front axle problems.

A clean engine bay like this makes it easier to spot leaks after a test drive.

The power of the V8 engine has advantages, but careful tuning for optimum fuel economy and the increased costs of spares are factors to consider.

Land Rover Defender mirrors can be fitted to the door hinges if rear visibility needs to be improved.

and may break a halfshaft if not released from four-wheel drive as soon as the problem is noticed. Note that engaging four-wheel drive on a tarred or concrete surface, where no wheel slip is possible, can cause an axle halfshaft to break.

The aluminium body panels don't corrode, except where they are joined to the chassis or other steel supports.

Be aware that the speedometer may not be original, and that off-road mileage is much more aging on the mechanicals than shopping trips around town.

Exterior

Check for corrosion at the bulkhead corners where the top front door hinges are mounted. Replacement welding sections are available for these areas. If the whole bulkhead is rusted, it's almost as costly as a chassis to replace.

A slight tilt on the vehicle to the driver's side is quite common, especially with short-wheelbase models. This is due to the fuel tank and driver being on the same side, which puts extra stress on those particular springs, eventually weakening them.

Check the two body-mounting points on the rear crossmember for an insight into the extent of electrolytic corrosion on the vehicle.

The nature and typical lifestyle of a Series Land Rover dictates that there are likely to be some scratches and dents to the bodywork. Many enthusiasts see these as simply recording previous skirmishes off-road. You need to decide upon your own level of acceptable previous adventure souvenirs.

Under-bonnet/hood

Is it the original engine? The 2286cc petrol and diesel engines prior to 1980 have a three-bearing crankshaft and run less smoothly and are less durable at motorway speeds than the five-bearing engines that succeeded them. The three-bearing diesel engine is prone to having the crankshaft flex and break at high revs. Can you see the engine number on the engine block? Does it agree with the one quoted in the registration document? Has off-road activity splashed battery acid around and caused serious corrosion to the battery and air filter supports or to the nearby chassis?

Underneath

All you need is a thin covering to spread on the ground to protect clothing and you can look underneath, because ground clearance is at least 8in (20cm), and significantly more than this in most areas.

Examine the chassis next to and to the rear of each wheel; these parts get the water, mud and stones thrown at them. A torch may be useful here, and don't forget to feel on top of the box chassis sections. Tapping the chassis firmly with a coin should give a clear metallic ringing sound on good metal, a dull thud indicates a corroded, sound-absorbing surface. Importantly, the chassis tends to rust from the inside, where the damage cannot be seen. Outriggers and the rear chassis crossmember are usually first to require repairing, so look for signs of welding there. Chassis outriggers are available as replaceable parts. Any welding should appear neat and well carried out, with equivalent thickness steel. Be wary of a chassis coated with thick underseal; these areas are best tested by prodding with a screwdriver. Overlaid welded patches often conceal chassis rot and are not looked upon favourably by roadworthiness inspectors.

Look for stains on the brake backplates, which could be due to either leaking brake fluid from a brake cylinder or oil from the axle hub seal. Also look for oil leaking from the front swivel

The angle of the rear spring hanger should be about 45 degrees to the horizontal; less (as shown here) means the spring has become weakened.

Parabolic springs will improve passenger ride comfort but reduce load carrying capacity.

hubs on the front wheels. The presence of oil on the transmission brake backplate indicates that the oil seal there is damaged. Oil leaks from the front of the engine and the flywheel housing are time-consuming to repair and involve higher labour charges. Expect to see some oil on the bottom of the gearbox and on the engine sump.

Interior

Lift the corners of the floor covering in the footwells and check for corrosion along the floor seams and the bottoms of the door pillars. Replacement footwells and door pillars are available for welding in.

If the general condition of the seating is not to your satisfaction, then this should not be a critical factor in deciding whether to buy or not. You can upgrade to County trim specifications if you wish to.

Replacement seating and authentic-to-original fabric is available for all Series III interiors.

Electrics

Has the vehicle been rewired with a new loom? Consider it a bonus if it has; they are available for all models (from Autosparks UK). The original bullet connectors tarnish and corrode and they usually work loose on cold, dark nights when it's raining. You don't have time to test the whole system, but looking at the wiring in the engine bay should give an immediate impression of how much attention the present owner has given to this important area of concern. If the wiring is original, you could need to replace it soon.

Try the wiper motor to see if it's too sluggish to be effective, but do it with the engine running, as voltage drops may affect performance. Wet the screen with the screen washers to view the effectiveness of the sweep.

A bonus, for those not craving true marque authenticity, would be if the points system in the distributor has been replaced by an electronic ignition system – several options are available. I remember a fellow enthusiast shaking his head in disbelief after my vehicle started first time after three days stood idle on a wet campsite.

Paperwork

Be aware that problem vehicles are often passed on quickly. What is the reason for sale? If, on inspection, the vehicle still interests you, then you need to check the vehicle registration certificate (V5C in the UK). The document details should match the vehicle you are inspecting, including engine number and chassis number. If you are examining the vehicle at a location that isn't the registered address of the vehicle, then you should be satisfied as to why that is the case. In the United Kingdom, the person named on the V5C is the registered keeper, and is not legally required to be the actual owner.

Chassis numbers are mostly located on the right-hand front spring hanger (otherwise known as the dumb iron). A replacement galvanized chassis will not have a number, neither will a replacement dumb iron, unless it has been re-stamped by the owner. An original chassis number plate should be present on the bulkhead.

If the vehicle has been modified significantly, check that these modifications are approved by the DVLA (for UK residents) so as to retain age-related road tax exemption for pre-1973 vehicles. Other countries also have restrictions on some vehicle modifications, so be sure that you purchase a road legal vehicle.

Is it worth staying longer?

• Is the colour what you expected or would you be able to live with it?
• Is the paintwork acceptable to you?
• Are you confident you can identify and repair any faults you have found, or do you need a second opinion?
• Are the main mechanical components in reasonable working order?
• Are any problems you have discovered reflected in the sale price?
• Is your heart ruling your head? Maybe you need to refer to a marque owner/ specialist, rather than act in haste and repent at leisure.

8 Key points
– where to look for problems

Key points are focussed around the problems that would cost the most to rectify. For all models, this involves thoroughly checking the chassis, bulkhead, engine and gearbox. Getting these items repaired professionally may require budgeting for more than the initial cost of the vehicle itself. If you are carrying out all the work yourself, it will be time-consuming and you may need to budget for specialist tools and lifting gear. However, the cost savings will be considerable. In some locations it may be possible to hire the necessary equipment. Some countries have low labour charges, but these can be offset by the cost of having bulky items shipped out to you from the UK or elsewhere.

Water thrown into the chassis dumb irons rots them from inside. Stress from the leaf spring accelerates the corrosion. This example is unroadworthy.

The chassis outriggers behind the wheels are most prone to corrosion; these support the body so good strength is vital.

The chassis will often rust from the inside, and the corrosion becomes visible along the bottom edges, as illustrated here.

The footwells and front door pillars form part of the bulkhead. These rot at their lowest points. Remove any floor covering to inspect this area thoroughly.

The corner bulkhead is very prone to corrosion. Replacement inserts are available for welding-in. Use a magnet in this area to test if body filler has been used in a repair.

Alloy bodywork corrosion can occur around all points where the steel chassis connects to the aluminium body panels.

If the rear chassis crossmember is covered in mud, scrape through it to inspect this area; it is very prone to corrosion.

Spring leaves should be parallel throughout their length. These leaves show some splaying apart, indicating weakness and increased risk of fracture.

9 Serious evaluation
– 60 minutes for years of enjoyment

Score each section as follows: 4 = excellent; 3 = good; 2 = average; 1 = poor
The totting up procedure is detailed at the end of the chapter. Be realistic in your marking!

It's hard to remember all the details of a vehicle you inspect, even an hour or two later, so tick the boxes in each section as you go along.

The evaluation procedure has been arranged with efficiency in mind. The intended inspection order is: external inspection, underneath examination from front to rear, under bonnet/hood inspection, internal assessment, test drive, and then finally, a follow-up assessment. If inspecting at a dealership, check if it has a hoist or ramp that you can use.

If professional repainting is required, then having the bodywork stripped down and surfaces repaired will be costly.

Paintwork ☐4 ☐3 ☐2 ☐1
You may wish to display the vehicle at classic vehicle or Land Rover shows and prefer a professional, authentic-to-the-year paint job. Or, working in a remote jungle area, brush-painted Hammerite may be sufficient for your needs. Probably, your requirements fall somewhere between these extremes. Decide upon what quality of paintwork is appropriate to your wishes and needs and score the vehicle accordingly. A professional paint job will last a long time, and could prove a good investment. If, however, you prefer to go down the DIY route, then year and model-specific paint is available to either spray, brush-on, or apply with a roller. You need a larger than average garage if you plan to do the painting yourself indoors. Many standard Series III models have been upgraded to County specification, with the characteristic County full-length body stripes added on. Genuine County Station Wagon models were available in only Russet Brown or Masai Red, with limestone upper panels. Whilst focussing upon paintwork, look for any areas where there is a mismatch of colour – suspect repairs and investigate further.
• Condition of paintwork

Check alignment along the line of body panel cappings. Problems may originate from poor assembly or a wrongly welded outrigger.

Body panels ☐4 ☐3 ☐2 ☐1
On Land Rovers of this age group, you are more likely to find dents than corrosion, as the body panels are aluminium alloy, which is weaker than steel. Body panels are secured to steel

Chequer-plate is commonly fitted for body protection and cosmetic effect. Removing it will leave holes to be filled.

frames, and yes, these frames do rust. Some panels are becoming harder to find, and plastic reproductions for some of them are becoming available.

Some alloy panels are fixed together with steel bolts, and these two dissimilar metals interact so that the alloy around the fixing point corrodes. This is often the reason why a wing panel, for example, may appear a little loose, resulting in it rattling on rough ground.

The traditional method of using a weak magnet to detect the presence of body filler will not work on the alloy panels. However, it's comforting to know that a panel will not have been body-filled because of corrosion problems, but simply to have saved the trouble of panel beating the metal back into shape – not easily achieved with Birmabright alloy, as it can become brittle.

• General condition of panels

Front wings/fenders ④ ③ ② ①

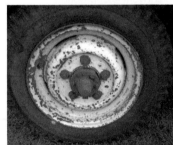

Not usually a problem area.
Check for corrosion of headlamp bowls fitted into the wings, as they are prone to road spray in this location. Plastic replacement bowls eliminate this problem. If

Wheelarch extensions can be added to legally accommodate larger tyres.

a front-mounted winch is fitted, check the security of its mounting.
• The mudshield at the rear of the wing for corrosion
• The mounting of the wing panels to the bulkhead pillars for security
• Radiator support frame for corrosion

Wheels ④ ③ ② ①

• With the axle safely supported on a stand, gripping a wheel at both sides and rocking it firmly will identify any play due to worn wheel bearings. If grasped at the top and bottom, any play will either confirm worn wheel bearings or, on front wheels, indicate worn swivel pins. Wheel bearings are time-consuming to replace but not expensive to buy.

Rusty wheels should be carefully inspected for structurally dangerous weakening at seams and around wheel nuts.

They can be replaced without specialist tools, though a hub bearing box spanner is useful
• If original steel wheels are fitted, check for corrosion along the central grooved depression, and check alloy wheels for cracking

This inner tube valve has been fitted with a spacer to protect it from rim hole abrasion. Check valves carefully.

• Check wheel nut mounting flanges on the spare wheel for severe corrosion. You'll have to assume the other four are in a similar condition

Tyres

235/70/R16 and 235/85/R16 are large enough and relatively fuel economical for short-wheelbase and long-wheelbase vehicles, respectively.

Aggressive tread gives good off-road performance but lowers fuel economy and makes for heavier steering.

A complete set of new tyres is a major expense. A mix of crossply and radial tyres on the same axle is dangerous and usually illegal.

• Assess the tyres relative to your intended use
• Are tyre treads legal, and walls without cracks?

Well maintained wheels and tyres like this are a bonus, as they represent a significant investment by the owner.

A wide range of aftermarket wheel rims are available, to which tubeless tyres may be fitted.

Windscreen

Its ability to fold flat across the bonnet provides a useful facility on all models in tropical climates. Usually, however, the hinges have long ago seized solid.
• The windscreen can fold flat against the bonnet/hood
• No glass damage in driver's vision

Door shut lines

Draughts around door edges are common, and can be a real problem in cold climates.

Stand at the rear of a closed door and look along the door line:
• Is there a uniform space down the vertical height of the door?
• Does a glazed door bend out a little at the top? This would indicate there is corrosion at the joint between the upper and lower sections of the door where they bolt together. Rear passenger doors on long-wheelbase models are especially susceptible to this fault. Mounting the spare wheel on the rear door of a Station Wagon can distort the door over time.

Difficult to get a draught-proof seal on a door as stressed as this.

Doors

The door skins are Birmabright alloy and will not show corrosion, except for where they contact the steel door frame. The internal frames and door pillars are steel and corrosion is common. If no trim is present, you can inspect the steel door frames.

Water can sit in the window channels, encouraging mould and rotting them. This

Doors may fly open on rough ground unless the locks are lubricated and correctly adjusted.

When the door joint rusts, the door top flexes and lets in rain.

rot progresses down the steel door frame. Replacement channels and complete door tops are available. Keeping drain holes clear under the windows is important.
• Inspect the surface of closing edges, especially where the lower and upper door sections join
• With a door half open, lift it up, feeling for wear in the hinges
• Feel along the bottom edges of the doors for corrosion. White powder indicates electrolytic corrosion between the aluminium door skin and the steel frame

Door trim

Replacement trim kits are available, even in the original look, grey 'elephant hide.'
Note: Many Series III Land Rovers don't have door trim, in which case assess the visible door frame instead.
• Assess the trim's condition, especially near the bottom where water may well have leaked inside the door

Replacement steel door frame sections can be cut to length and welded-in as required.

Lock barrels can be replaced if faulty – no need for a complete lock replacement.

Hinges are strong and resistant to wear. But, if worn, they are not serviceable and must be replaced.

The sill channels/rockers

These are hidden from view by the body sill panels. They are subject to rotting, especially at the ends. In four-door models, check under the middle door pillar. Replacements are available but time-consuming to weld-in.
• General condition

Body attachment points

These can be seen without getting underneath the vehicle. You will probably find some corrosion here, but it should only be minor and around the points where the aluminium body is joined to the chassis. Measures were taken at the design stage to minimize this electrolytic corrosion by using various materials to separate the two interacting metals.

• Inspect where the rear body is bolted to the rear chassis crossmember

• Also where the centre body is bolted to chassis outriggers on long-wheelbase models

Here, body attachment points had corroded the alloy flooring. Repair work was carried out using aluminium angle iron.

Door pillars

Water rots them from inside the channels, especially the bottom ends (see photo Chapter 8). Replacement pillar sections are available to be welded-in.

• Examine the regions above and below where the hinges are attached on all side doors

• Also the sloping part of the pillar on rear side passenger doors on 109in Station Wagon models

Flooring

For any flooring that is thick aluminium alloy and is screwed down check:

• Areas around the floor panel fixing screws for corrosion of the panels or of their steel mating surfaces

• The horizontal alloy flanges on the seat base for corrosion caused by a combination of stress and the steel fixing screws

• The footwells on driver and passenger sides for corrosion, especially along seams and where bolted to the floor panels

• The lower edges of the steel gearbox diaphragm cover

Replacing corroded flooring panels with aluminium chequer-plate is a common option to resolve flooring problems.

Corrosion of the steel gearbox diaphragm cover can be obscured by floor covering.

Check underneath any floor covering for corrosion.

Gearbox tunnels are prone to rusting, but panels are readily available and easily fitted.

Bulkhead/dash ☑4 ☑3 ☑2 ☑1

If this is badly corroded then walk away, unless you are looking for a major restoration project and the vehicle is being offered at a giveaway price. Replacement sections for footwells, front door pillars and windscreen corner sections are available off-the-shelf for welding-in. Any other corrosion will involve metal fabrication prior to welding, or an expensive complete bulkhead replacement (see Chapter 8 for photos).
Check:

• The upper footwell area (not checked earlier)
• Internally, the area between the windscreen and door pillar on driver and passengers side
• The area just below the windscreen (difficult to repair)
• The external corners just below the windscreen on each side of the vehicle

Checking under the vehicle ☑4 ☑3 ☑2 ☑1

Series III models can be inspected from underneath, without lifting gear, due to their large ground clearance. Walk around the vehicle first and look for marked tilting of the body to one side, or sagging at the front or rear, indicating weakened leaf spring(s). Be aware that the vehicle may have been used off-road, so check for collision damage underneath.

A 3ft (1m) wide piece of carpet, or similar, helps keep clothes clean, though overalls are advisable.

Even in daylight, a torch is useful for inspecting darker corners.

Chassis ☑4 ☑3 ☑2 ☑1

The steel used on Series III Land Rovers was often not of the same quality as on earlier Series I, II & IIA models, so check carefully. If the original chassis is still fitted, try to find and read the chassis number (usually on the right-hand side front dumb iron) – read as many consecutive digits as possible and note them down. If a galvanised chassis has been fitted, it's a large bonus.

Tapping the chassis with a small screwdriver and listening for a metallic ring or dead thud reveals the state of the chassis, as much internally as externally. Corrosion tends to occur from the inside, since moisture stays there longer. Some visible chassis repairs are likely to be seen.

Off-roading can cause chassis dents, and crossmembers can become bent. Be aware, whilst

It was common in the UK in the 1970s to 'upgrade' Series III models to coil spring suspension. Kits were available to do this.

checking under the vehicle, that loose and hanging brake pipes can lead to stress fractures, so look out for any. If the chassis drain holes are blocked, internal chassis corrosion is more likely.

Check the following on each side of the vehicle (see Chapter 8 for photos):

- Front dumb iron
- Rear spring hanger brackets (109in models in particular)
- Integrity of any visible repairs, such as welded patches
- Outriggers
- The lowest parts of the chassis
- Sides and top around the rear wheel areas (especially near the bump stops)
- Rear crossmember and attached rails (88in models in particular). Especially important if you plan to tow

Front axle

Rusted leaf springs will cause a harsh ride. Corrosion is most serious at the ends of the leaves, and it can cause them to fracture. A thin film of oil between the spring leaves helps reduce friction and corrosion, indicating a dedicated owner. Rubber shock absorber bushes and spring bushes harden in time, especially in hot climates.

- Rear spring hangers of the front axle should be almost vertical, with the individual leaves of each spring all parallel to each other, not splayed apart
- Any sign of oil or brake fluid stains on the lower part of a brake backplate indicates a leaking oil seal or faulty brake cylinder
- If the chrome swivel hubs on the front axle are not hidden by leather gaiters, their surfaces should be smooth not pitted. There shouldn't be oil leaking from the large seal, as evidenced by oil having reached the lower swivel arm fixing bolts. Sand and mud trapped under the swivel seal erodes the chrome surface. Leaking hubs can be concealed by using swivel hub grease.

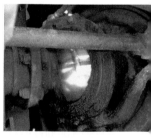

Protection of swivel hubs by leather gaiters is a bonus.

Standard fitting to the 109in model only, the Salisbury axle (seen here) is stronger than the alternative Rover axle.

Chrome swivel hubs are expensive to replace and time-consuming to fit. They leak oil if the surface is pitted.

Oil leaks

It's common for the lower engine sump area to display signs of oil leaking from somewhere. It's a good idea to wipe the area clean after inspecting it and then check again after the test drive. Be aware that off-roading damage may be the cause of some oil leaks. The following sources of oil leak are more difficult and costly to repair:

- From behind the crankshaft pulley at the front of the engine
- From the rear lower surface of the cylinder head
- Where the front propshaft joins the differential housing

Steering

For this you need to lay under the vehicle, with the wheels on the ground, whilst someone turns the steering wheel from side-to-side; but not enough to actually turn the wheels themselves as you will stress the system. Do this repeatedly, until you have finished carrying out the checks:

• There should be no movement at all between the swivel pin housing and the swivel steering lever at the point where they are bolted together
• No free movement in any of the six steering assembly ball joints
• No oil leaking out of the bottom of the steering relay

A steering damper is a bonus. If the wheels shake after hitting a pothole, the damper's shock absorber needs changing.

Shock absorbers

There's no practical way of testing these whilst on the vehicle, except that you can look for leakage of oil on the sides of them.

If the shock absorber has oil on it, check it hasn't simply been blown on from a leaking axle joint.

Gearbox

Check for oil leaks in the following places:
• A slight amount from the drain hole in the flywheel housing is not unusual, but it means that the crankshaft rear oil seal will need attention in the future – an expensive repair in terms of labour charges
• Oil on the lower gearbox is usually coming from the oil filler cap, as it's only held down by a spring and the cork joint washer often doesn't give a good seal
• Any oil around the junction of the front propshaft with the gearbox will be coming from the front output shaft oil seal
• Oil stains on the drum of the transmission brake means the rear output shaft oil seal is leaking, and this oil could get onto the transmission brake linings. This seal is time-consuming to replace

Propshafts

• With freewheel hubs engaged (if fitted), there should be less than a quarter-turn of free play on the front propshaft
• With handbrake off and wheels choked, perform the same test on the rear propshaft
If more than a quarter-turn is observed, costly general transmission wear may be the cause, particularly in the differential.

A worn universal joint will show movement between the yoke and the joint when a screwdriver is used as a lever between them.

Rear axle

It's okay if spring leaves are horizontal, but not bent downwards. Radial tyres all around and parabolic springs improve ride-ability, especially on short-wheelbase models, although parabolic springs can reduce load carrying capacity.

Perform these checks for each end of the axle:

• Rear spring hanger should be at approximately 45 degrees and individual leaves of the spring of uniform thickness, all parallel to each other and not splayed apart

• Any signs of oil or brake fluid stains on the lower part of the brake backplate indicates a leaking oil seal or faulty brake cylinder

The Rover axle and standard leaf springs, as shown here, are common on non-military Land Rovers.

Emission control connections should not leak, especially in countries where emissions for Series III models are regulated.

Fuel tanks(s)

Water-contaminated fuel or condensation in an empty tank can cause corrosion from the inside. Off-road driving with perished rubber tank mountings can stress corroded seams and cause leakage – in the case of petrol, detectable by smell, rather than by sight. Tanks are not practical to repair, and rear tanks can be expensive to replace.

• Check for leakage

Exhaust system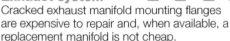

Cracked exhaust manifold mounting flanges are expensive to repair and, when available, a replacement manifold is not cheap.

• Check the entire system for corrosion and good flexible mountings. Only award an 'Excellent' rating if a stainless steel system is fitted

• Inspect the inside of the tailpipe for a powdery black deposit, indicating an over rich fuel mixture, or a dark greasy deposit that indicates a worn engine. Ideally, it should be light grey

Several companies in the UK convert Series Land Rovers to LPG for better fuel economy. DIY kits are also available.

Mechanical aspects

If the spare wheel is mounted on the bonnet, check the security of the fastenings on the bonnet prop rod before poking your head inside the engine bay. If no wheel is mounted there, it's only a few seconds job to disconnect the prop rod and hold the bonnet back against the windscreen for easier inspection.

Cooling system

If there is water movement in the radiator neck on starting a cold engine, the thermostat is missing or jammed open.

• Check for signs of water leaking through the vanes of the radiator or from the top and bottom sealing joints. This is best done before the engine is warm

• Remove the radiator cap and look for any oil film; if present, the cylinder head gasket is probably about to fail

• When the engine is off, feel under the top fan belt pulley for water from a leaking water pump

Top right: Check condition of heater water hoses and the large bore air supply hose for tight fitting and leaks.

Right: White deposits splattered around the engine bay indicate that the cooling system is leaking.

Replacing the mechanical fan with an electric version is okay for economy in cool climates, but not in tropical countries.

Engine & ancillaries

If a V8 engine has been installed, check that brakes and suspension have been suitably upgraded to match the increased performance. If an alternative engine has been fitted, ask who carried out the work, and assess the workmanship as best you can. Is it an engine for which spare parts are readily available.

The post-1980 2286cc engines are smoother running and less inclined to crankshaft failure at high revs, due to them having five main bearings instead of three. Cast iron cylinder heads on diesels are prone to cracking, and a sign of this is air bubbles in the coolant when the radiator cap is removed. **Do not** remove the radiator cap when engine is hot!

Cylinder heads are either 7:1 or 8:1 compression ratio, and are interchangeable on the 2286cc petrol engine. The ratio is stamped on the cylinder head. The six-cylinder engine tends to wear its exhaust valves (lack of power and possible backfiring), and the aluminium cylinder head is subject to distortion and corrosion. The six-cylinder engine is the same as that found in 3-litre Rover saloon cars.

The bush in which the throttle spindle rests wears eventually and causes fuel to leak. Leaks here are not usually repairable.

- On petrol engines, check the carburettor spindle for wear by turning it and wriggling it in all directions. If sideways movement is present, the carburettor will leak fuel and needs replacing – the Zenith fitted as standard is prone to this fault
- If you are aiming at an authentic restoration according to year and model, then check what parts you may wish to replace, even though they may be perfectly serviceable at present; parts such as the air cleaner, carburettor and oil filter

Miscellaneous engine bay mechanicals

- Check that the steering box and relay are both securely attached to the chassis and not leaking large amounts of oil
- An oil cooler may have been fitted by a previous owner. Check for leaks, and be aware that this engine has probably had a hard life at some point in the past, as oil coolers are not required for normal operation

While looking in the engine bay, make a note of the engine number. It's stamped vertically on a smooth section of the engine block, near the exhaust outlet and the water pump housing.

Do you need to replace non-standard parts that may conflict with your personal preference for authenticity? The K&N filter shown here can increase performance.

Check the oil filler cap and rocker cover air vent for signs of oil being blown out, which suggests worn engine components.

The wiring loom

Electrical problems are common on older vehicles, as the insulation becomes brittle and cracks, and the bullet and spade end connections become corroded and work loose. Amateur installations are common, and should be treated with scepticism.

New looms are available for all models from Autosparks (www.autosparks.co.uk). Distributors can be expensive to repair, and cheap replacements aren't reliable.

- The main loom and all its extensions should be secured to the body, engine or chassis, as appropriate, to prevent chafing
- If the loom is the original wiring, score poor for this section
- Additional wires for added instruments or extra lighting, etc, should have been fitted with secondary insulation in a similar manner to the main loom, and be of the correct electrical load rating.

Additional wiring that may have been added should have been routed away from sources of heat and moving parts.

Unleaded or LPG conversion

For petrol engines, ask to see written evidence that the cylinder head has had the original valve seats removed, and hardened valve seats inserted. New valves should have been fitted at the same time – it's a costly conversion. Failure to convert the seats will shorten the life of the cylinder head. It takes several thousand miles before deterioration in engine performance becomes apparent, though. DIY LPG conversion kits are available, but the conversion should have been checked and approved by an accredited authority – ask for written evidence of this.

* Evaluate the quality of the conversion, if carried out

Chassis & engine number

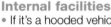

Petrol and diesel 2286cc engine blocks are interchangeable, but petrol and diesel crankshafts are not the same strength. A diesel engine could have a petrol engine block number, no problem. It's important however, to ensure that the crankshaft of a diesel engine does not have a 'P' stamped on it; signifying it's for petrol engine use only. Unfortunately, this isn't a very practical check, as it requires the engine sump to be removed first.

The engine number on the 2286cc engine is stamped vertically on the engine block, next to the exhaust manifold.

* It's now time to enter the vehicle. Does the number here match that on the chassis (you may have made a note of this earlier) and agree with the one recorded on the vehicle registration document?

Note that VIN plates are also available as blanks, so inspect the plate for age characteristics. The UK's V5C form is printed on paper having distinctive watermarks to deter forgery, so check this if the VIN plate looks suspiciously new.

The VIN plate is usually fixed to the bulkhead above the gearbox tunnel, but location does vary and it may be hidden by aftermarket sound insulation.

Internal facilities

* If it's a hooded vehicle and the hood is available, make sure you see it fully erected and check it for tears, stains and secure fitting
* If seat belts are fitted (not a legal requirement in pre-1973 UK registered vehicles), check condition of the belts and mountings – faults mean a road test certificate failure

Not evident here, but shrinkage is a common problem with hoods that have not been well cared for. They cannot be stretched back to original size.

Headlinings are often damaged due to condensation. Easier to clean than replace this Safari roof lining.

- Has a sound insulation kit been fitted (a bonus on diesels)? If yes, and it has been stuck down to the floor, then mark down, as it restricts floor inspection
- Any switches, instruments or other control items obviously damaged?

Internal aesthetics   4 3 2 1

If you are purchasing for serious off-road use, don't allow a neat and tidy interior trim to eclipse the significance of any mechanical failings that you may have already spotted. On the other hand, if you are developing a liking for the vehicle but the interior or soft hood is poor, be aware that these trim items are all available, even in original, authentic-style, if required, although placing orders to UK suppliers from overseas countries will increase costs.

Exmoor Trim can supply material for DIY seat renovation, refurbish seats, or supply replacements.

- Is the relatively basic interior to your taste, or will you need to upgrade/renovate it?

Test drive

Provided you are insured and the vehicle is road legal, take it for a 30 minute test drive. This is the only satisfactory way to assess some important mechanical aspects of the vehicle. If you are only insured for third party claims, then you may wish to inform the seller of this fact.

Engine start   4 3 2 1

The present owner will best advise on throttle and/or choke settings according to present weather conditions.
- Does the starter gear engage fully with the flywheel? Does it sound like there is a worn starter cog, or even missing flywheel teeth?
- Does the engine start easily? Be aware that a pre-warmed engine (prior to your arrival) will likely start first time

The Zenith 36IV carburettor is standard for the 2.25-litre engine. It's difficult to restore to reasonable fuel economy when faulty.

Engine sounds   4 3 2 1

The 2286cc petrol engine is known to suffer from timing chain rattle. Diesel engines need about 30 seconds of glow plug preheating to start. The 2286cc petrol engine has a reputation for outliving its diesel counterpart.
- The engine should idle reasonably smoothly; allowing for accumulated wear in moving components. If you feel it's a little too erratic, check it again after the test drive. A multi-meter with tachometer capability is useful here for checking smooth running. Uneven idling is often carburettor related
- If there is a metallic rattle from the top of the engine, indicating tappet problems, check again after the test drive. If still present, then mark down, but this problem is not usually expensive or difficult to fix. In 2286cc engines especially, the noise could also be due to cam followers or worn camshaft
- Listen for dull knocking sounds from low in the engine. If present, worn crankshaft bearings, or even a worn crankshaft, is likely. Both petrol and diesel 2286cc

A rough-running engine could be due to a loose exhaust connection at the manifold end. Can you rattle the pipe when it has cooled down?

three-bearing engines (pre-1980) tend to wear the centre crankshaft bearing due to flexing of the crankshaft at high revs
• Check the exhaust smoke when the engine is revved a little from idling, and again during and after the test drive: if continuous and blueish, then pistons and/or rings are worn; if black, fuel mixture is rich for petrol, or the injection system needs an overhaul for a diesel (can be expensive). Intermittent bluish smoke may just be perished valve stem oil seals

If the engine does not rank highly on this section and you found oil leaks in the earlier 'oil leaks' test then it's probably time to walk away now. 2286cc engines have a long life and can struggle on when wear is obviously apparent.

Lights   4 3 2 1

• Switch on the headlamps and check the reading on the ammeter (if present) as you do so. The ignition warning light should remain off and not glow, provided no other electrical items are on at the same time
• Do all the other lights/indicators work?

Headlamp bowls are subject to corrosion. Plastic alternatives are available.

Additional lighting is a bonus, as 25+ year old headlight design does not suit modern day driving conditions.

Instruments/warning lights   4 3 2 1

• The standard instruments are very basic and limited in scope. It's common for owners to have added oil pressure and perhaps other additional gauges themselves. Check the effectiveness of all gauges fitted, and use their information to assess the engine's condition as you continue through the test drive
• The green oil warning light should illuminate with ignition on and quickly extinguish when the engine starts. If no oil pressure gauge is fitted, check whether or not the oil warning light is glowing when the engine is idling; if so, an engine rebuild is required
• If a heater is fitted, check the fan operates. You could check the amount of heat produced during or after the test drive. They are not known for their effectiveness in heating the interior

Dashboard ancillary items 4 3 2 1

Before setting off on the test drive, check the operation of the windscreen wipers and screen washers.
Check the sweep of the blades and the speed of the wiper motor (engine running).

Additional instrumentation can be added using bespoke Series III panels from Classic Land Rover Accessories (www.classiclandrover.co.uk)

Optional extra items 4 3 2 1

Possibilities include (not all models): heated windscreen, fly screens and a radio.
• Assess whatever extras are present

Loose fitting or perished brake vacuum piping can cause more brake pedal pressure to be required.

Brake pedal operation 4 3 2 1

If you are not satisfied with the first two brake checks, don't continue with a test drive.
• The brake pedal should be firm on initially applying pressure and should not travel more than halfway to the floor before stopping
• Check the brake master cylinder seals by repeatedly pressing gently on the brake pedal. A good seal will allow the pedal to come to rest at the same point each time. Also apply continuous pressure on the pedal and see if the pedal gradually creeps down at all, or remains firm

If brake troubles are due to a problem with the internal brake servo, be aware that these units are not repairable.

Poor brake performance could be due to leaking fluid. It's often easily spotted, as here, by checking the brake backplates.

If you purchase the vehicle, it's recommended that you thoroughly inspect the braking system on each wheel in case a problem is developing.

• Do the brakes inspire confidence? Do they require excessive pedal pressure? Bear in mind whether or not the vehicle you are inspecting has servo assisted brakes. Not all models do, though servo assisted brakes were fitted as standard on 109in and six-cylinder models.

Note that all models can be converted to servo assisted, if desired
• Does the vehicle stop in a straight line? If not, it could be due to a partially seized brake cylinder or fluid on the brake linings
• Any scraping sounds on braking suggests badly worn brake linings. Note that temporary brake squeal, heard on braking, is common when the brake drum edges are corroded and grit gets inside the brake drum. Brake fade can be due to glazed brake linings and polished brake drums. The glaze can be broken as a cure, instead of replacing components

Clutch assessment ④ ③ ② ①
• Depress the clutch pedal to the floor. There shouldn't be a squealing sound, which could indicate a worn clutch release bearing. They are cheap to buy but expensive or time-consuming to fit
• If first gear is difficult to select, a worn clutch is possible, but it could also be worn gear selector forks
• Does the clutch engage when the pedal is about halfway up its travel arc? The clutch is self-adjusting on all models, though it needs setting up correctly initially

If the drain plug was in place here, it could obscure an oil leak from the crankshaft oil seal.

• Does the clutch engage smoothly without juddering? If juddering is experienced, it could be a clutch problem or loose engine/gearbox mountings
• If vehicle speed does not increase in relation to increased throttle, the clutch is worn and slipping

Gearbox assessment ④ ③ ② ①
Ease of gear selection can be tested with the vehicle stationary and the transfer lever in neutral. Note that gear changes need to be made more slowly than with modern vehicles. The gearbox is not as strong as those found on earlier Series I, II and IIA models.
• Does the gearbox sound chattery on over-run in any gear, suggesting a worn gearbox?
• Are there any knocking sounds when the vehicle is reversed?
• Does the gearbox jump out of any gear when releasing the accelerator suddenly after accelerating? This could be a synchromesh problem

These are indications of general gearbox wear. A replacement gearbox is usually more economical than a complete overhaul, though DIY overhaul kits and workshop manuals are available.

If freewheel hubs are fitted, you will need to engage these before you can test the four-wheel drive.

Four-wheel drive
As mentioned earlier, the only

sure way to test this is to find a loose, gravely surface and see if the front wheels spin.
• Check both high and low transmission gearboxes. There shouldn't be any unhealthy sounds. If four-wheel drive cannot be selected, it will probably be a linkage problem

Steering

'Clonk' sounds from a front wheel on turning sharp corners could be loose U-bolts or worn suspension bushes.
• Does the vehicle steer straight without the need for constant correction? Some adjustment for slackness is available on the steering box, but it could be due to worn swivel hubs or bearings. Note that if crossply tyres are fitted, the steering will tend to follow grooves in the road. Remember that steering needs to pass the test for a roadworthiness certificate. Steering boxes can be expensive to replace or recondition
• Does the steering self-centre after cornering? This indicates that the swivel hub bearings are lubricated
• It's quite common for quite violent shaking to occur after hitting a pothole on models where a steering damper is not fitted. Steering damper kits are available

Transmission/parking brake

• If a gentle slope and a steep incline are available, try the former first for handbrake efficiency. Otherwise, with high ratio first gear selected and the handbrake on, try moving off gently. If forward movement is possible, either oil from the gearbox has contaminated the transmission brake linings or the mechanism needs adjustment
• Park on a decline, and then release the transmission brake. If there is reluctance to move forwards then the transmission shoes can be binding. Check again using the brake pedal, and if the same occurs then the wheel brake shoes are binding. The latter is easily verified by feeling for warmth in the steel wheels after a short drive

Curing a slipping handbrake due to leaking oil requires time-consuming replacement of an oil seal.

Curing a slipping handbrake ratchet just requires adjustment, or this pawl replacing.

Overdrive

Series III Land Rovers had the option of a factory-fitted Fairey overdrive unit, which became obsolete but is now remanufactured. These units were also obtainable from

the manufacturer, and subsequently fitted by many owners of Series III models. Secondhand units are often seriously worn, and new parts are now available. Rocky Mountain makes a Roverdrive to fit these models. If an overdrive is fitted and is working satisfactorily, mark as Excellent.

Fairey overdrives like this were an optional factory fitting. These are now being remanufactured and parts are available.

Performance assessment

If an observed reduced performance is traceable to the Zenith 36IV carburettor, then good quality replacements are hard to find. Switching to a Weber 34ICH is an alternative that will increase fuel economy but slightly reduce power.

• Did the engine rev well at the top end of the range, indicating a well tuned ignition system, or fade off and lose power too early?

• Given a suitable stretch of level road, it should be possible to reach 60mph with all petrol models that are in good condition and well tuned. Diesels should be able to reach 55mph if well tuned

It is important to check fuel lines for leaks on a diesel engine. Painting them like this makes the job easier.

Seating

• On completion of the test drive, evaluate how you felt regarding comfort, ease of operation of the controls, and all

Even Range Rover seating can be fitted to a long-wheelbase model (as shown here), but your engineering skills will be tested.

round visibility. It's easiest to fit alternative seating to Station Wagon models. Remember that seating installation must satisfy requirements of a road safety test. More comfortable Series III County model seating can be fitted to all models. Damage to County seating is more expensive to repair/ replace than standard seating.

Unlike Series I, II and some IIA models, Series III Land Rovers are legally required to have seat belts fitted in the UK.

Engine health
Leave the engine running and check:
• That tappets are not significantly noisier than they were on idling before the test drive
• Remove the oil vent cap from the rocker cover and check for a creamy deposit, indicating a head gasket problem
• For signs of oil splattering from the oil filler cap when the engine is revved, and for back pressure at the rocker cover vent – both indicating a worn engine

External aesthetics
The vehicle may be still baring off-road driving scars. If it's a soft top model, check if the perspex windows have become brittle and cracked.
• Is the front bumper damaged?
• Are the rear corners damaged?
• Are the wheels standard and in good condition or, if alloy rims have been fitted, will these suit any off-road requirements you may have?

Mud flaps may improve rear visibility in some driving conditions.

Ancillary equipment
A wide variety of possible off-road or utility equipment may have been fitted, such as: a winch, roof-rack, tow hitch, chequer-plate body panels, underbody

If a winch is fitted, you need to be sure it works, unless the seller declares that it requires repairing.

These original-style steps are very popular and are now remanufactured.

protection guards, additional lighting, etc.
• Score the equipment present according to its condition and particular appeal to you

Roadworthy test certificate
You need to see the most recent roadworthy test certificate and check if any recommendations for further improvement have been recorded on it. Note that the number of countries prohibiting the registration of older vehicles for use on public roads is increasing.

A variety of tow hitches are available. They all impose a reduced departure angle when off-roading.

Evaluation procedure
Add up the total points.
**Score: 204 = excellent;
153 = good; 102 points = average; 51 = poor.**
A vehicle scoring over 143 should be completely usable and require the minimum of repair, although continued maintenance and care will be required to keep it in condition. Vehicles scoring between 51 and 104 will require full restoration; the cost of which will be much the same regardless of points scored. Vehicles scoring between 105 and 142 points will require very careful assessment of the necessary repair/restoration costs in order to arrive at a realistic purchase price.

www.velocebooks.com / www.veloce.co.uk
Details of all current books • New book news • Special offers

10 Auctions
– sold! Another way to buy your dream

Auction pros & cons

Pros: Prices should be lower than those of dealers or private sellers and you might grab a real bargain on the day. Auctioneers will usually have established clear title with the seller. It is often possible to examine documentation relating to the vehicle at the venue.

Cons: You have to rely on a sketchy catalogue description of condition and history. The opportunity to inspect is limited and you cannot drive the vehicle. Auction vehicles are often a little below par and may require some work. It's easy to overbid. There will usually be a buyer's premium to pay in addition to the auction hammer price.

Which auction?

Auctions by established auctioneers are advertised in car magazines and on the auction houses' websites. A catalogue, or a simple printed list of the lots for auction might only be available a day or two ahead, although lots can be listed and pictured on auctioneers' websites much earlier. Contact the auction company to ask if previous auction selling prices are available, as this is useful information (details of past sales are often available on websites).

Catalogue, entry fee & payment details

When you purchase the catalogue of the vehicles in the auction, it often acts as a ticket allowing two people to attend the viewing days and the auction. Catalogue details tend to be comparatively brief, but will include information such as 'one owner from new, low mileage, full service history,' etc. It will usually also show a guide price to give you some idea of what to expect to pay and detail what is charged as a buyer's premium. The catalogue will also contain details of acceptable forms of payment. At the fall of the hammer an immediate deposit is usually required, the balance payable within 24 hours. If you plan to pay by cash, note that there maybe a cash limit. Some auctions will accept payment by debit card, and sometimes credit or charge cards are acceptable, but will often incur an extra charge. A bank draft or bank transfer will have to be arranged in advance with your own bank as well as with the auction house. No vehicle will be released before all payments are cleared. If delays occur in payment transfers then storage costs can accrue.

Buyer's premium

A buyer's premium will be added to the hammer price – don't forget this in your calculations. It's not unusual for there to be a further state tax or local tax on the purchase price and/or on the buyer's premium.

Viewing

In some instances it's possible to view on the day, or days before, as well as in the hours prior to the auction. Auction officials may be willing to help out by opening engine and luggage compartments and allowing you to inspect the interior. While the officials may start the engine for you, a test drive is out of the question. Crawling under and around the vehicle as much as you want is permitted, but you can't suggest that the vehicle you are interested in be jacked up, or attempt to do the job yourself. You can also ask to see any documentation available.

Bidding

Before you take part in the auction, decide on your maximum bid – and stick to it!

It may take a while for the auctioneer to reach the lot you are interested in, so use that time to observe how other bidders behave. When it's the turn of your vehicle, attract the auctioneer's attention and make an early bid. The auctioneer will then look to you for a reaction every time another bid is made; usually the bids will be in fixed increments until the bidding slows, whereupon smaller increments will often be accepted before the hammer falls. If you want to withdraw from the bidding, make sure the auctioneer understands your intentions – a vigorous shake of the head when he or she looks to you for the next bid should do the trick!

Assuming that you are the successful bidder, the auctioneer will note your card or paddle number, and from that moment on you will be responsible for the vehicle.

If the vehicle is unsold, either because it failed to reach the reserve or because there was little interest, it may be possible to negotiate with the owner, via the auctioneer, once the sale is over.

Successful bid

There are two more items to think about – how to get the vehicle home and insurance. If you can't drive the vehicle, your own or a hired trailer is one way, another is to have the vehicle shipped using the facilities of a local company. The auction house will also have details of companies specialising in the transfer of vehicles.

Insurance for immediate cover can usually be purchased on site, but it may be more cost-effective to make arrangements with your own insurance company in advance, and then call to confirm the full details.

eBay & other online auctions

Buying online could land you a vehicle at a bargain price, though you'd be foolhardy to bid without examining the vehicle first; something most vendors encourage. A useful feature of eBay is that the geographical location of the vehicle is shown, so you can narrow your choices to those within a realistic radius of home. Be prepared to be outbid in the last few moments of the auction. Remember, your bid is binding and that it will be very, very difficult to get restitution in the case of a crooked vendor fleecing you – caveat emptor!

Be aware that some vehicles offered for sale in online auctions are 'ghost' vehicles. Don't part with any cash without being sure that the vehicle does actually exist and is as described (usually pre-bidding inspection is possible).

Auctioneers

Barrett-Jackson www.barrett-jackson.com Bonhams www.bonhams.com British Car Auctions BCA www.bca-europe.com or www.british-car-auctions.co.uk Cheffins www.cheffins.co.uk Christies www.christies.com Coys www.coys.co.uk Dorset Vintage and Classic Auctions www.dvca.co.uk eBay www.eBay.com www.eBay.co.uk H&H www.classic-auctions.co.uk RM www.rmauctions.com Shannons www.shannons.com.au Silver www.silverauctions.com

11 Paperwork
– correct documentation is essential!

The paper trail
Classic, collector and prestige vehicles usually come with a large portfolio of paperwork accumulated and passed on by a succession of proud owners. This documentation represents the real history of the vehicle and from it can be deduced the level of care the vehicle has received, how much it's been used, which specialists have worked on it and the dates of major repairs and restorations. All of this information will be priceless to you as the new owner, so be very wary of vehicles with little paperwork to support their claimed history.

Registration documents
All countries/states have some form of registration for private vehicles whether its like the American 'pink slip' system or the British 'log book' system.

It is essential to check that the registration document is genuine, that it relates to the car in question, and that all the vehicle's details are correctly recorded, including chassis/VIN and engine numbers (if these are shown). If you are buying from the previous owner, his or her name and address will be recorded in the document: this will not be the case if you are buying from a dealer.

In the UK the current (Euro-aligned) registration document is named 'V5C,' and is printed in coloured sections of blue, green and pink. The blue section relates to the car specification, the green section has details of the new owner and the pink section is sent to the DVLA in the UK when the car is sold. A small section in yellow deals with selling the car within the motor trade.

Previous ownership records
Due to the introduction of important new legislation on data protection, it is no longer possible to acquire, from the British DVLA, a list of previous owners of a car you own, or are intending to purchase. This scenario will also apply to dealerships and other specialists, from who you may wish to make contact and acquire information on previous ownership and work carried out.

If the car has a foreign registration, there may be expensive and time-consuming formalities to complete. Do you really want the hassle?

Roadworthiness certificate
Most country/state administrations require that vehicles are regularly tested to prove that they are safe to use on the public highway and do not produce excessive emissions. In the UK that test (the 'MOT') is carried out at approved testing stations, for a fee. In the USA the requirement varies, but most states insist on an emissions test every two years as a minimum, while the police are charged with pulling over unsafe-looking vehicles.

In the UK the test is required on an annual basis once a vehicle becomes three years old. Of particular relevance for older cars is that the certificate issued includes the mileage reading recorded at the test date and, therefore, becomes an independent record of that car's history. Ask the seller if previous certificates are available. Without an MOT the vehicle should be trailered to its new home, unless you insist that a valid MOT is part of the deal. (Not such a bad idea this, as at least you will know the car was roadworthy on the day it was tested and you don't need to wait for the old certificate to expire before having the test done.)

In the UK, vehicles over 40 years old on May 20th each year, are exempt from MOT testing. Owners can still have the test carried out if they so wish.

Road licence

The administration of every country/state charges some kind of tax for the use of its road system, the actual form of the 'road licence' and, how it is displayed, varying enormously country to country and state to state.

Whatever the form of the road licence, it must relate to the vehicle carrying it and must be present and valid if the car is to be driven on the public highway legally.

Changed legislation in the UK means that the seller of a car must surrender any existing road fund licence, and it is the responsibility of the new owner to re-tax the vehicle at the time of purchase and before the car can be driven on the road. It's therefore vital to see the Vehicle Registration Certificate (V5C) at the time of purchase, and to have access to the New Keeper Supplement (V5C/2), allowing the buyer to obtain road tax immediately.

In the UK, classic vehicles 40 years old or more on the 1st January each year get free road tax. It is still necessary to renew the tax status every year, even if there is no change.

If the car is untaxed because it has not been used for a period of time, the owner has to inform the licensing authorities.

Certificates of authenticity

It's possible to get a certificate proving the age and authenticity (eg engine and chassis numbers, paint colour and trim) of a particular vehicle, these are called Heritage Certificates and if the vehicle comes with one of these, it's a definite bonus. If you want to obtain such a certificate, go to www.heritage-motor-centre.co.uk.

If the vehicle has been used in European classic car rallies, it may have a FIVA (Fédération Internationale des Véhicules Anciens) certificate. The so-called 'FIVA Passport' or 'FIVA Vehicle Identity Card' enables organisers and participants to recognise whether or not a particular vehicle is suitable for individual events. If you want to obtain such a certificate go to www.fbhvc.co.uk or www.fiva.org, there will be similar organisations in other countries, too.

Valuation certificate

Hopefully, the vendor will have a recent valuation certificate, or letter signed by a recognised expert stating how much he or she believes the particular vehicle to be worth (such documents, together with photos, are usually needed to get 'agreed value' insurance). Generally, such documents should act only as confirmation of your own assessment of the vehicle rather than a guarantee of value, as the expert has probably not seen the vehicle in the flesh. The easiest way to find out how to obtain a formal valuation is to contact the owners' club.

Service history

Often these vehicles will have been serviced at home by enthusiastic (and hopefully capable) owners for a good number of years. Nevertheless, try to obtain as much service history and other paperwork pertaining to the vehicle as you can. Naturally, dealer stamps, or specialist garage receipts score most points in the value stakes.

However, anything helps in the great authenticity game; items like the original bill of sale, handbook, parts invoices and repair bills adding to the story and the character of the vehicle. Even a brochure correct to the year of the vehicle's manufacture is a useful document and something that you could well have to search hard to locate in future years. If the seller claims that the vehicle has been restored, then expect receipts and other evidence from a specialist restorer.

If the seller claims to have carried out regular servicing, ask what work was completed, when, and seek some evidence of it being carried out. Your assessment of the vehicle's overall condition should tell you whether the seller's claims are genuine.

Restoration photographs

If the seller tells you that the vehicle has been restored, expect to be shown a series of photographs taken while the restoration was under way. Pictures taken at various stages, and from various angles, should help you gauge the thoroughness of the work. If you buy the vehicle, ask if you can have all the photographs, as they form an important part of its history. It's surprising how many sellers are happy to part with their vehicle and accept your cash, but want to hang on to their photographs! In the latter event, you may be able to persuade the vendor to get a set of copies made.

12 What's it worth?

– let your head rule your heart

Condition

If the vehicle you are considering is in such obviously bad condition that the assessments in Chapter 7 or 9 weren't necessary, either make sure it has all the parts on it that you need to extract, or that it provides a sufficiently robust basis for a restoration project. Further advice on restoration is given in Chapter 13.

If you did use the marking system in chapter 9 you'll know whether the car is in Excellent (maybe concours), Good, Average or Poor condition.

The monthly Land Rover magazines run regular price guides. If you haven't bought the latest editions, do so now and compare their suggested values for the model you are thinking of buying. Also look at the auction prices they're often reporting. Values have been fairly stable for some time, but some models will always be more sought-after than others. Trends can change, too. The values published in magazines tend to vary a little from one magazine to another, as do their scales of condition, so read carefully the guidance notes they provide. Bear in mind, a vehicle that is truly a recent show winner could be worth more than the highest scale published. Assuming that the vehicle you are considering is not in show/concours condition, relate the level of condition that you judge the vehicle to be in with the appropriate guide price. How does the figure compare with the asking price? Before you start haggling with the seller, consider what affect any variation from standard specification might have on the vehicle's value. If you are buying from a dealer, remember there will be a dealer's premium on the price.

Desirable options/extras

For collectors, who are concerned with having the vehicle closely resemble its assembly line condition, factory-fitted desirable options could be a Fairey overdrive unit or hydraulic drum/capston winch, a front or central power take-off unit, towing equipment or an oil cooler. These are most of the main assembly line optional extras available for early Series III vehicles (most were available from Series I onwards actually). A wide variety of other factory-fitted options became available in the ensuing years for Land Rovers covered by this guide. Collectors may need to establish whether any of these particular later options were available at the time of manufacture for a specific year model.

For non-collectors, their interests may be more focussed upon the suitability of the vehicle to match their requirements. You may require enhanced off-road capability or increased comfort over the standard spartan factory-fitted interior. Accessories available include: electric winch, rock sliders, underbody protection plates, parabolic springs, chequer-plate body panels, electronic ignition, additional lighting, alloy wheels, LPG conversion, weber carburettor, electric fan, a raised air intake or a more powerful engine. Personal preferences vary enormously, so a non-collector may not regard some of the above options/extras as desirable.

Series III Land Rovers are much less economical to run than modern 4x4s and this needs to be well understood by any potential buyer, so any cost saving additions or modifications may appear desirable. In the UK, any Series III vehicle first registered prior to 1st January 1973 will be exempt from paying annual road tax. Very few of these are around now, however, and there is a need to check the authenticity of any potential pre-1973 model. A conversion to use LPG fuel or the addition of an overdrive unit will significantly reduce fuel consumption.

Undesirable features

Any body part which introduces a visible hybrid characteristic to the vehicle, such as running boards being fitted from another 4x4 instead of the standard Land Rover side steps, or Land Rover Series II hinges on a Series III model. Some hardtop van-sided Series III models have had aftermarket rear side windows fitted rather than go to the expense of fitting a Station Wagon rear body. This may make a future sale less attractive to some potential buyers.

Engine conversions from later model Land Rovers (eg the Discovery range) are popular, but conversion to a non-Land Rover engine is considered less desirable by many enthusiasts.

Striking a deal

Negotiate on the basis of your condition assessment, vehicle mileage, and fault rectification cost. Also take into account the vehicle's specification. Be realistic about the value, but don't be completely intractable; a small compromise on the part of the vendor or buyer will often facilitate a deal at little real cost. Get a receipt for any cash that exchanges hands, and be sure that all the relevant vehicle documents are in your possession, including any relating to change of ownership, and that they are legitimate.

13 Do you really want to restore?
– it'll take longer and cost more than you think

Define 'restore'

Do you want to restore a vehicle to roadworthy condition, or do you want to return it to how it may have appeared just after leaving the factory? It took me six months to restore my Series Land Rover sufficiently to get it through its roadworthiness certificate. It had simply stood idle and unattended on grass for several years. Improvements continue.

Bob Lane's Series III 109in Station Wagon prior to restoration. (Courtesy Bob Lane)

Practicality

A Series Land Rover was designed for ease of maintenance and repair. Many mechanical parts are serviceable and appropriate repair kits are available, as opposed to requiring off-the-shelf new replacements.

Time allocation

It will take you longer than you think. Having both a full-time job and a Land Rover restoration leaves little time for anything else. Decide whether you should work on those aspects that will allow you to get it to a roadworthy state

Bob's fully-restored Series III on display at a Land Rover show in the UK. (Courtesy Bob Lane)

first, or jump in at the deep end, and commit to a plan that leaves the vehicle unusable until project completion. If you are hoping to work over a winter period, less daylight hours may be available and you will require adequate indoor lighting and heating.

Economics

Restoration is not economical, even if you do all the labour yourself. Expect professional

The best source of used parts in the UK is at the various Land Rover shows that run from April to September.

restoration costs to greatly exceed the purchase price of the vehicle. You will not recover your investment, no matter how concours the restoration is, but what price can you put on achievement?

Space
Restoration requires lots of it; preferably indoors, otherwise you will be weather dependent. Do you have this space available yourself or courtesy of a friend, or could you rent it economically? When compelled to work outdoors with limited hard standing, I have found a large sheet of 10mm plywood useful as a base for the lifting crane when removing the engine or gearbox. The width of the plywood is dictated by the distance between the front wheels. At least some work can then be done indoors.

Logistics
Can you realistically source all the parts required, in the order needed, as financing allows and according to the projected schedule? If you are held back whilst waiting for parts, your schedule crumbles. You may need to pay more for parts to get them quickly, rather than wait for the free postage option from local suppliers. A parts catalogue for your vehicle is very useful, as it reduces the risk of ordering the wrong part.

Be prepared for the unexpected; you can't know this wheel is scrap until you've removed it and seen the corroded stud hole.

Human resources
'More hands make light work,' so is there any help available? Potentially inconvenienced family members and neighbours need to be supportive of your endeavours.

Tools/equipment
A variety of specialist tools, such as torque wrench and engine hoist, will be required. If you don't already have these and can't borrow them as required, then you need to budget for the purchase or hire of them. If restoration involves welding, do you have the equipment and the skills required?

Allow sufficient time for freeing seized bolts. Shearing a bolt causes delay. Neither a local workshop nor a replacement part may be available.

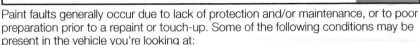

14 Paint problems
– bad complexion, including dimples, pimples and bubbles

Paint faults generally occur due to lack of protection and/or maintenance, or to poor preparation prior to a repaint or touch-up. Some of the following conditions may be present in the vehicle you're looking at:

Orange peel
This appears as an uneven paint surface; similar to the appearance of the skin of an orange. The fault is caused by the failure of atomized paint droplets to flow into each other when they hit the surface. It's sometimes possible to rub out the effect with proprietary paint cutting/rubbing compound, or very fine grades of abrasive paper. A respray may be necessary in severe cases. Consult a bodywork repairer/paint shop for advice.

Orange peel.

Cracking
Severe cases are likely to have been caused by too heavy an application of paint (or filler beneath the paint). Also, insufficient stirring of the paint before application can lead to the components being improperly mixed, and cracking can result. Incompatibility with the paint already on the panel can have a similar effect. To rectify it's necessary to rub down to a smooth, sound finish before respraying the problem area.

Cracking.

Crazing
Sometimes the paint takes on a crazed rather than cracked appearance when the problems mentioned under Cracking are present. This problem can also be caused by a reaction between the underlying surface and the paint. Paint removal and respraying the problem area is usually the only solution.

Blistering
Almost always caused by corrosion of the metal beneath the paint. Perforation will usually be found in the metal and the damage will be worse than that suggested by the area of blistering. The metal will have to be repaired before repainting.

Corrosion blistering caused by interaction between the steel door frame and the aluminium alloy door skin.

Micro blistering

Usually the result of an economy respray where inadequate heating has allowed moisture to settle on the vehicle before spraying. Consult a paint specialist, but damaged paint will have to be removed before partial or full respraying. Can also be caused by car covers that don't 'breathe.'

Fading

Some colours, especially solid reds, are prone to fading if subject to strong sunlight for long periods without polish protection. Sometimes proprietary paint restorers and/or paint cutting/rubbing compounds will retrieve the situation. Often a respray is the only real solution.

Peeling

Often a problem with metallic paintwork starts when the sealing lacquer becomes damaged and begins to peel off. Poorly applied paint may also peel. The remedy is to strip and start again!

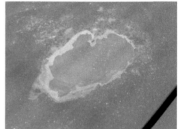

Peeling lacquer.

Dimples

Dimples in the paintwork are caused by the residue of polish (particularly silicone types) not being removed properly before respraying. Paint removal and repainting is the only solution.

Dents

Small dents are usually easily cured by Dentmaster, or an equivalent process, that sucks or pushes out the dent (as long as the paint surface is still intact). Companies offering dent removal services usually come to your home – consult your telephone directory or the web.

Dimples.

15 Problems due to lack of use
– just like their owners, Land Rovers need exercise!

Vehicles, like humans, are at their most efficient if they exercise regularly. A run of at least ten miles (17km) once a week is recommended.

Seized components
• Pistons in brake/clutch, slave and master cylinders can seize
• The clutch plate may bond to the flywheel and seize if left unused for months
• Handbrakes (parking brakes) can seize if the linkages rust
• Pistons can seize in the bores due to corrosion

Marks on this clutch lining show it had bonded to the flywheel and would not release due to flywheel corrosion.

Fluids
• Old, acidic oil can corrode engine bearings
• Uninhibited coolant can corrode internal waterways. Lack of antifreeze can cause core plugs to be pushed out, even cracks in the block or head. Silt settling and solidifying can cause overheating
• Brake fluid absorbs water from the atmosphere and should be renewed every two years. Old fluid with a high water content can cause corrosion and pistons/calipers to seize (freeze), and also brake failure when the water turns to vapour near hot braking components
• Fuel with an alcohol component also contains water that can cause corrosion in the fuel tank

Additives in modern fuel degrades it over time. The tank can be emptied via the drain plug. Dispose of fuel in an environmentally-friendly way.

Steel cup (Welch) plugs in the engine block can corrode from the inside and develop pinhole leaks.

Tyre problems

Tyres that have had the weight of the vehicle on them in the same position for some time will develop flat spots, resulting in some (sometimes temporary) vibration. The tyre walls may also have cracks or (blister-type) bulges, meaning new tyres are needed.

Shock absorbers (dampers)

With lack of use, the dampers will lose their elasticity or even seize. Creaking, groaning and stiff suspension are indicators of this problem.

Rubber & plastic

Radiator hoses may have perished and split, possibly resulting in the loss of all coolant. Window and door seals can harden and leak. Gaitors/boots can crack. Wiper blades will harden, causing them to be detached easily from their arm mountings. The diaphragm in the distributor's vacuum advance can harden, resulting in retarded ignition timing – leading to a hotter than normal engine, risk of burnt values and a waste of fuel.

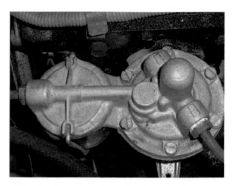

The diaphragm on mechanical fuel pumps can harden and then tear when used. Overhaul kits are available.

Electrics

• The battery will be of little use if it has not been charged for many months
• Earthing/grounding problems are common when the connections have corroded. Old bullet and spade type electrical connectors commonly rust/corrode and will need disconnecting, cleaning and protection (eg: Vaseline)
• Sparkplug electrodes will often have corroded in an unused engine
• Wiring insulation can harden and fail

Rotting exhaust system

Exhaust gas has a high water content, so exhaust systems corrode very quickly from the inside when the car is not used.

Springs/suspension

Moisture will cause the leaves of leaf springs to rust and bond together, causing a harsh ride and increasing the risk of fracture. Rubber spring bushes will harden and contribute to a harsh ride.

Grass is the worst ground to stand a vehicle on as it constantly releases moisture into the air.

16 The Community
– key people, organisations and companies in the Land Rover world

Clubs
UK

Approximately 100 local and national Land Rover clubs. Details on the UK clubs page of www.series123.com Land Rover Series III & 90-110 Owners' club www.thelandroverclub.co.uk

Europe & some parts of the world

Details on the links page of www.lrfaq.org/FAQ.5.clubs.europe.html

Australia & New Zealand

Clubs throughout both countries. Details on the clubs page of www.series123.com/AUS/

The Series 3 & 90-110 Owners Club is UK-based, but has a worldwide membership.

USA & Canada

Clubs in at least 26 states and 5 provinces. Details on the clubs page of www.series123.com/USA/

Main spares suppliers
UK

John Craddock Ltd North Street, Bridgtown, Cannock, Staffordshire WS11 0AZ Tel: + 44 (0)1543 577207 Fax: +44 (0) 1543 460160 Email: general@johncraddockltd.co.uk, Web: www.johncraddockltd.co.uk
Dunsfold DLR Alfold Road, Dunsfold, Surrey, GU8 4NP Tel: +44 (0) 1483 200567 Fax: +44 (0)1483 200738 Email: dlr@dunsfold.com Web: www.dunsfold.com
Pegasus Parts Surrey Email: pegasusparts@btinternet.com Web: www.pegasusparts.co.uk

USA

Rovers North Inc 1319 Vermont Route 128, Westford, VT USA 05494-9601 Tel: 1-802-879-0032 Web: www.roversnorth.com
British Pacific 26007 Huntington Lane, Unit 2, Valencia, California 91355 Tel: 1-800-554-4133 Web: www.britishpacific.com

Canada

3 Brothers Classic Rovers Paris, Ontario. Tel: 519-302-3227 Email: Sales@3BrothersClassicRovers.com Web: www.3brothersclassicrovers.com

Australia
British Off-road 7069 Chevallum Road, Forest Glen, Sunshine Coast, Queensland 4555 Tel: 61 7 5445 1094 Email: enquiries@britishoffroad.com Web: www.britishoffroad.com

Refurbished Land Rovers
Liveridge British 4x4 Ltd export refurbished and used Land Rovers worldwide: Valley Farm, Valley Road, Earlswood, Solihull, West Midlands, B94 6AA Tel: +44 (0)1564 703 682 Web: www.liveridge4x4.com

Magazines & books

Classic Land Rover Key Publishing Ltd, PO Box 300, Stamford, Lincolnshire, PE9 1NA Web: www.classiclandrover.com

Land Rover Monthly Dennis Publishing Ltd, Bedford Technology Park, Thurleigh, Bedford, MK44 2YP Web: subscribe.lrm.co.uk

Land Rover Owner International Bauer, Media House, Lynchwood, Peterborough PE2 6EA Web: www.lro.com

Land Rover Diesel Series IIA and III 1958-85 Service and Repair Manual (Haynes Service and Repair Manuals) by JH Haynes and John S Mead ISBN: 1859601790

Land Rover Series III Repair Operation Manual (Workshop Manual Land Rover) [Illustrated] [Paperback] Brooklands Books Ltd ISBN 1855201089

Land Rover Series III Owner's Manual (1979-85 MY) (Owners Handbook) [Illustrated] [Paperback] by Brooklands Books Ltd ISBN 1855202263

Land Rover Series III Reborn [Illustrated] [Paperback] by Lindsay Porter Veloce Publishing Ltd ISBN 1845843479

Land Rover Series 3 Parts Catalogue [Paperback] by Brooklands Books Ltd ISBN 1855202131

Land Rover Series III Specification Guide [Hardcover] by James Taylor The Crowood Press Ltd ISBN 1847973205

Land Rover Series 3 4x4 Performance Portfolio 1971-1985 (Brooklands Books Road Test Series) (Performance portfolio series) [Illustrated] [Paperback] by RM Clarke; Brooklands Books Ltd ISBN 1855204762

Land Rover Series 3, 1971-85 (Brooklands Books Road Tests Series) by RM Clarke. Brooklands Books Ltd; ISBN 1869826043

www.velocebooks.com / www.veloce.co.uk
Details of all current books • New book news • Special offers

Production history

1971 first Series III vehicles produced
1974 Land Rover exports to USA and Canada cease
1976 one millionth Land Rover produced
1980 five-bearing 2286cc petrol/diesel engine introduced
1982 County Station Wagon launched
1985 final Series III models produced

Load capacities

88in

Model	Min unladen weight	Max allowable weight
Soft top petrol	2856lb (1298kg)	4664lb (2120kg)
Soft top diesel	2939lb (1336kg)	4664lb (2120kg)
Cab truck petrol	2875lb (1307kg)	4664lb (2120kg)
Cab truck diesel	2959lb (1345kg)	4664lb (2120kg)
Hard top petrol	3181lb (1446kg)	4664lb (2120kg)
Hard top diesel	3271lb (1487kg)	4664lb (2120kg)
7-seater Station Wagon petrol	3357lb (1526kg)	4664lb (2120kg)
7-seater Station Wagon diesel	3447lb (1567kg)	4664lb (2120kg)

109in (4-cylinder engines)

Model	Min unladen weight	Max allowable weight
Soft top petrol	3540lb (1609kg)	5962lb (2710kg)
Soft top diesel	3648lb (1658kg)	5962lb (2710kg)
Cab truck petrol	3546lb (1612kg)	5962lb (2710kg)
Cab truck diesel	3654lb (1661kg)	5962lb (2710kg)
Hard top petrol	3639lb (1654kg)	5962lb (2710kg)
Hard top diesel	3747lb (1703kg)	5962lb (2710kg)
12-seater Station Wagon petrol	3967lb (1803kg)	5962lb (2710kg)
12-seater Station Wagon diesel	4050lb (1841kg)	5962lb (2710kg)

The 'payload' is the load (excluding the driver and 1 passenger) that a vehicle may reasonably be expected to carry comfortably cross-country. It's generally around 1000lb (460kg) throughout the model range, except for the 1500lb (680kg) of the 109in '1-ton'.

Fluid capacities

	2286cc	2625cc
Cooling system	10.2-litre (petrol)/2.7gal (US) 9.9-litre (diesel)/2.6gal (US)	11.3-litre/3gal (US)
Engine sump (including filter)	7.1-litre/1.9gal (US)	7.3-litre/1.9gal (US)
Gearbox	1.5-litre/3.2pts (US)	1.5-litre/3.2pts (US)
Transfer box	2.5-litre/5.3pts (US)	2.5-litre/5.3pts (US)

Swivel hubs   0.6-litre/1.3pts (US)
Differential
Rover   1.7-litre/3.6pts (US) (front & rear)
Env   1.4-litre/3pts (US) (rear) 1.2-litre/2.5pts (US) (front)
Salisbury   2.5-litre/5.3pts (US) (front & rear)

Fuel tanks: All fuel tank capacities are 10gal (45-litre/11.9gal[US]), except for the 109in six-cylinder and 109in Station Wagon that are 15gal (68-litre/18gal [US]).

Spark plugs
2.25-litre: 7:1 compression: Champion N8; 8:1 compression: Champion N12Y
2.6-litre: Champion N5

Ignition timing
2.25-litre engine
7:1 compression: 6 degrees BTDC
8:1 compression: 0 degrees TDC
8:1 compession (emission controlled): 6 degrees ATDC

2.6-litre engine
7:1 compession: 6 degrees BTDC
8:1 compression: 2 degrees ATDC
Ducellier distributor dwell angle is 57 degrees

Valve clearances
2286cc petrol/diesel: inlet and exhaust 0.010in (0.25mm) hot or cold
2625cc petrol: inlet 0.006in (0.15mm); exhaust 0.010in (0.25mm) hot

Turning circle
88in: 38ft (11.6m) **109in:** 47ft (14.3m). Larger tyres increase the turning circle.
Toe-in: $\frac{3}{64}$in (1.2mm) to $\frac{3}{32}$in (2.4mm)
Wheel nuts (Series III splined studs): 80lb.ft/108Nm; 10.3-11.7kg.m

Tyre sizes
88in: 6.00-16, 6.50-16, 7.00-16 or 7.50-16in **109in:** 7.50-16in

Tyre pressures (loaded and unloaded)
Front 25lb/in^2 (1.76kg/cm^2/1.72BAR) for all models and all listed tyre sizes
Rear 30lb/in^2 (2.11kg/cm^2/2.07BAR) for 88in and 36lb/in^2 (2.53kg/cm^2/2.48BAR) for 109in
For more comfort on roads, rear pressures can be reduced to 25lb/in^2 (1.76kg/cm2/1.72BAR) for 88in and 30lb/in^2 (2.11kg/cm^2/2.07BAR) for 109in.

Fuel consumption
88in 2286cc petrol 18mpg, diesel 28mpg
109in 2286cc petrol 17mpg, diesel 26mpg
109in 2625cc petrol 14mpg
Sustained urban use will lower these figures. Use of four-wheel drive dramatically reduces them.

Land Rover's coil-sprung models include the first-generation Range Rover, One Ten family, Defender family and first-generation Discovery models. All have been taken into service by the British armed forces, and this unique book describes and illustrates their uses and adaptations, while containing comprehensive vehicle lists and contract details.

ISBN: 978-1-787112-40-7
Hardback • 25x25cm
144 pages • 275 pictures

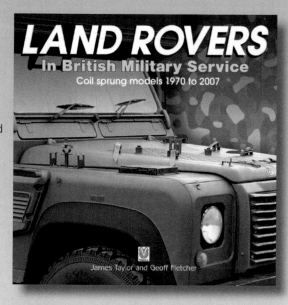

This book tells the story of the use of Land Rovers by the emergency services over a period of nearly 70 years. Examples of the major conversions for Fire, Police and Ambulance use are featured, showing how the different types have been adapted for these specialist roles.

ISBN: 978-1-787112-44-5
Hardback • 25x25cm
144 pages • 275 pictures

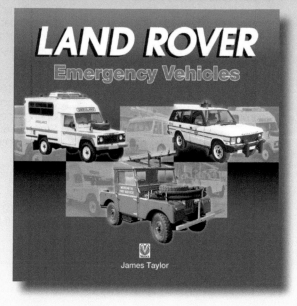

www.velocebooks.com *or email us at* info@veloce.co.uk

Index